Dedicated to

My Elder Brother (*Late*) **Dr.** *Deepak Kumar Srivastava (1975–2007)*

Quotes of my dearest brother who always inspire me to do best-

"Philosophy is never ending,

It needs a better thought,

Every time and can be appended,

If it will fitted with the,

Principle and doctrine of the concept"

&

"Putting anything on test is good,

But imperfect representation always mislead the way"

And

My Parents *Mrs. Asha Srivastava & Mr. K.P. Srivastava*

'A drop of water is worth more than a sack of gold to a thirsty man'

– Anonymous

Contents

Preface   *ix*

Chapter I   **Water Pollution**   **1**

1.1 Characteristics of Water   2

1.2 Types and Sources of Water Pollution   11

1.3 Industrial Wastes   24

1.4 Heavy Metals and Water Pollution   29

1.5 Thermal Pollution   34

1.6 Water Microbiology   35

1.7 Water Analysis and Analytical Methods   36

Chapter II   **Water Treatment Process**   **41**

2.1 Introduction   41

2.2 Layout for Treatment Plants   43

2.3 Industrial waste Water Treatment   58

2.4 Purification of Water   59

2.5 Pattern of Water Supply in Rural Areas   71

2.6 Pattern of Water Supply Projects   72

Chapter III   Sewage and Sewage Treatment Process   **75**

  3.1 Introduction   75

  3.2 Resolution of Sewage Treatment Plant   76

  3.3 Method of Collection of Sewage   76

  3.4 Sewage Disposal   80

  3.5 Characteristics and Examination of Sewage   83

  3.6 Sewage Treatment Processes   93

  3.7 Miscellaneous Methods of Sewage Treatment Processes   95

Chapter IV   Self-Purification of Natural Water   **99**

Chapter V   Effluent Treatment Plant (ETP) and Sewage Treatment Plant (STP)   **101**

  5.1 General Introduction   101

  5.2 Effluent Treatment Plant   109

  5.3 Sewage Treatment Plant (STP)   119

Chapter VI   Water Management   **127**

  6.1 Introduction   127

  6.2 Need of Water Management   129

  6.3 Rainwater Harvesting   134

  6.4 Water Management for Industrial Waste and Municipal Sewage Waste   138

  6.5 Water Management for Agriculture   142

  6.6 Water Management at Household   147

Chapter VII Policy Dimension   **149**

7.1 Introduction   149

7.2 Millennium Development Goals and Water Resources   151

7.3 Sustainable Development Goal (SDG) and Water Resources   153

7.4 Water Scarcity – A Challenge   157

7.5 Author Point of View   160

7.6 Conferences on Water Security   162

Bibliography   165

Tables:

Table 1.1 Physical properties of water are as following;   3

Table 1.2 Status of pollution of lake in India   17

Table 1.3 Status of River Polluted in India.   21

Table 1.4 Sources, Impact of heavy metal on health.   31

Table 1.5 indicates the conversion of ppm to ppb.   37

Table 1.6 MPN of Coliform organism existing in 100 mL of water
(Source: Dubey & Maheshwari, 1999).   40

Table 2.1 Water Quality Standard   44

Table 2.2 Comparison between Trickling Filter and Activated Sludge Process   54

Table 2.3 Water Borne Diseases   60

Table 3.1 depicts the comparison between conservancy and water-carriage system.   78

Table 5.1 Quality Standards for Inlet Effluent of Common Effluent Treatment Plant.   102

Table 5.2 Quality Standard for Treated Effluent of Common Effluent Treatment Plant   102

Table 5.3 Water Quality Standard (as per IS 10500–1991)   104

Table 5.4 Treatment and Mechanism of ETP   114

Table 6.1 Annual Groundwater Extraction by Countries as per 2010 Report.   129

Table 7.1 National Water Security Index and Scores (Sources: AWDO, 2016)   156

Figures

Figure 1.1 Sechhi Disk – Instrument to measure water transparency   10

Figure 1.2 Use of Secchi disk for finding water transparency   11

Figure 2.1 Flow Chart – Waste Water Treatment   46

Figure 6.1 Seriousness of climate change impact   132

Box

Box 1.1 Key Facts   16

Box 1.2 Status of lakes   17

Box 1.3 Water Analysis – Key Factors   36

Box 2.1 Water Supply Structure   41

Box 2.2 Comparison of Standard and High Rate filter   53

Box 2.3 Features of Treatment Process   57

Box 3.1 Flow Chart of the Process of Sanitary Works.   75

Box 3.2 Composition of Sewage   76

Box 3.3 Sewage Disposal   80

Box 5.1 Factors to be considered for planning an ETP.   110

Box 5.2 Flow Chart of Design of ETP   112

Box 6.1 Relationship between Supply and Demand   128

Box 6.2 System of Rainwater harvesting   137

Box 6.3 Recommended water recycling and application   140

Box 7.1 The Water Goals and its Targets   154

Preface

The book presented describes about the menace of water pollution in surface and groundwater resources. It further focused on the available treatment technologies for wastewater and comprehensively discuss about the status of water along with all possible and available technologies for the management of water resources. Therefore, the topic of this book entitled 'Wastewater Treatment and water management.' The last Chapter of this book throws light on policy dimension taken to preserve and conserve water resources and I have also given my own viewpoint on these policies concerning environment. This book briefly highlights and compiles the water treatment process as well as emphasis on the need of water management.

The sequence I have followed is to introduce the readers to the background, and impact of water pollution, the characteristic of water, its types and sources, and pollution arises due to industries, heavy metals, domestic, agriculture etc. As a consequences of water pollution in terms of various water borne diseases and further analysis of water pollution, are all mentioned in Chapter I: Water Pollution, followed by Water treatment process in Chapter II; Wastewater Treatment Process. This takes the reader to the discussion on the layout for treatment process; industrial wastewater treatment, purification of water and supply of water in rural and urban areas are all discussed in it.

The Chapter III: Sewage Treatment Process introduces readers to the method, pattern, and collection of sewage and sewage disposal. Further the characteristic and examination of sewage and various sewage treatment processes, such as, primary, secondary, and tertiary treatment processes are discussed in detail. Along with this, the layout of sewage treatment plant and miscellaneous methods of sewage treatment process, such as, oxidation pond, aerated lagoons, oxidation ditch, anaerobic lagoons, septic tank, and Imhoff tanks are comprehensively discussed in this Chapter.

This book further advances with Chapter IV: Self-purification of Natural water, this throws light on the natural capacity of water bodies to purify themselves, followed by Chapter V: ETP and STP, this introduces readers to all the factors which are considered for planning ETP and STP as well as their mechanism and design to treat effluents.

Further this takes readers to various ways of water management in Chapter VI: Water Management, that discuss about the requirement of water management at present scenario and the impact of Climate Change on water resources. This Chapter focused on the methods available to manage water resources, such as, Rainwater harvesting, then management of water at industries, agriculture, and domestic sector.

This book finally concluded with Chapter VII: Policy Dimension, which throws light on water policies adopted at world level, focusing on India, to protect, conserve, and manage water resources, briefly discussing Millennium and Sustainable Development Goals. Further this also highlights my own viewpoint on these policies in Section: Author's point of view.

CHAPTER I

Water Pollution

'Pollution is anything that goes against the principle of environment.'

– Dr. Anamika Srivastava

(Source: Google website)

Water is an essential constituent of all living matter. It is distributed in nature in varied forms such as rain water, spring water, river water, and mineral water. Everywhere water is required for various purposes. Civilization develops near water habitats. The huge dependency on water resources for survival led to the development of public water system. Water which is essential for survival; also a good carrier of disease germs, and may be responsible for water borne diseases. It is therefore necessary to ensure the right quality and quantity of water. After studying this chapter, one should be able to understand;

- The characteristics of water,
- Types and Sources of water pollution,
- Industrial wastes and water pollution,
- Heavy metals and water pollution,
- Thermal pollution,
- Water Microbiology, and
- Water analysis and analytical methods.

1.1 Characteristics of Water

1.1.1 Chemistry of Water

Water has high specific heat, which is responsible for preventing large fluctuations in the surface temperature of the earth, which is essential for the survival of aquatic organisms. Besides, high heat of vaporization of water is responsible for maintaining the earth's temperature relatively constant. Approximately one third of the solar energy which reaches the surface of the earth is dissipated by vaporizing water from ocean, river, lakes, and ice-fields. Water possesses the highest heat of fusion and heat of evaporation, collectively known as *latent heat*. The latent heat of water moderates the temperature of the biosphere. It plays significant role in the evaporation of water and its condensation as rain and as dew in the hydrological or water cycle. The surface tension of water is highest among all common liquid, except mercury. This higher surface tension plays a significant role in the movement of water through and into the organisms. Water is a poor thermal conductor and has high viscosity which permits organisms to swim using relatively simple movements. It also protects aquatic organisms from the mechanical disturbance. Further the expansion of water on freezing is advantageous as well as disadvantageous too. Extreme winter condition damages plants and animal tissues due to expansions of water, an essential constituent of all animals and vegetable matter, this eventually causes cell wall to burst. On the other hand, on the surface of the earth, the same process causes the breakdown of rocky materials to yield fertile soil. Water is considered to be an excellent and cheap solvent due to the following reasons:

- It has high dielectric constant,
- It is hydrogen bonded,
- It is polar molecule and has dipole movement.

Being excellent solvent, al natural elements are soluble in water, at least in trace amounts, and they are all found in natural water at some place or the other on the earth's surface. Thus water is the main medium by which chemical constituents are transported from one part of an ecosystem to the other. Organisms living at sea level experience a pressure at about 15psi. Pressure increases with increasing depth of water at the rate of one atmosphere for every 10 meters of descent. The solubility, ionic dissociation, and surface tension are all influenced by the pressure. Water is slightly compressible with increased pressure.

The sea water contains a dilute electrolyte solution in which principle solute species are Na^+, Cl^-, K^+, Ca^{2+}, Mg^{2+}, SO^{2-}_4, HCO_3^-, and Br^-. Besides, thousands of organic molecules and inorganic ions are present in trace amount in sea water.

1.1.2 Physical Properties of Water

Table 1.1 Physical properties of water are as following;

1	Boiling Point (°C)	100
2	Melting Point (°C)	0
3	Critical Temperature (°C)	374.20
4	Molar heat of vaporization (KJ)	40.67
5	Molar heat of vaporization (Kcal)	9.7
6	Molar heat of fusion (KJ)	6.02
7	Molar heat of fusion (Kcal)	1.44
8	Molar Entropy of Vaporization (Jdeg^{-1})	109
9	Molar Entropy of Vaporization (Cal/deg)	26.1
10	Viscosity at 20 °C (Centipoise)	1.005
11	Surface tension at 20 °C(dynes/cm)	73
12	Dielectric constant	80.54
13	Dipole moment (debye)	1.84
14	Specific heat (cal g^{-10}c^{-1})	1
15	Heat of Evaporation (cal/g)	540

1.1.3 Quality of Natural Water

The substances which are present in natural or raw waters can be broadly categorized into the following three groups;

- Coarsely dispersed or Suspended Substances
- Colloids and Molecular Substances
- Ion Dispersed Substances

1.1.3.1 Coarsely Dispersed Substances

These substances are particles of sand and clay of varied sizes, fragments of plants and other substances. These substances enter into the surface water-rivers, lakes, ponds by rain water or thawed snow. The maximum concentrations of these substances are usually observed during floods. In the raw water analysis, generally the amounts of impurities contained in a unit volume of water (ml/L) are determined.

1.1.3.2 Colloidal Substances

These are the substance of both organic and inorganic origin present in water in colloidal states. The humic substance (organic origin) found in great amounts in swamps waters impart a yellow to brown tinge. Contamination of raw waters by organic substances is mainly due to following two reasons–

- Dying of and decaying of organisms dwellings in water, and
- Discharge of untreated waste water by industries into water reservoirs.

Besides the inorganic substances such as rain, silicon, aluminum compounds are also present in water in colloidal state. These inorganic colloidal impurities hinder the performance of boiler units by increasing the tendency of boiler water foaming. Further, they also disturb the performance of anion exchangers that are irreversibly sorbing the anions of organic substances.

1.1.3.3 Ion dispersed or Molecular Dispersed Substances

These include salts and gases that are dissolved in water. The salts are usually dissociated to a large extent in aquatic solution, therefore, cation such as Na^+, Ca^{2+}, Mg^{2+} and anions such as Cl^-, SO_4^{2-}, HCO_3^- etc. are usually found in natural waters.

Natural waters generally contains compounds such as $Ca(HCO_3)_2$, $Mg(HCO_3)_2$, $CaCl_2$, $MgCl_2$, $CaSO_4$, $MgSO_4$, $NaSO_4$, $NaCl$. Besides they also contains nitrite acid ions, NO_2^- (nitrites), nitrous acid ions, NO_3^- (nitrates) and ammonium cation (NH_4^+) in trace quantities. But the presence of these nitrogen compounds in water is an indicator that water basin is contaminated by either industrial waste waters or by decomposition products of organic substances.

Ferrous compounds, usually in the form of ferrous bicarbonate, $Fe(HCO_3)_2$ is present in underground waters. These iron compounds are stable only in presence of large amount of CO_2 and hinders boiler heating surfaces by foaming a precipitation capable of scaling. For deferrization of ground water, CO_2 is removed from waste by blowing air through it. When the air is blown through the water containing iron, it causes the decomposition of $Fe(HCO_3)_2$, followed by the formation of ferrous hydroxide, $Fe(OH)_2$. The $Fe(OH)_2$ thus formed is oxidized by air or oxygen into $Fe(OH)_3$ which is removed from the water after its precipitation.

The presence of soluble gases such as oxygen and carbon-di-oxide in natural waters causes corrosion of metals. Thus, treatment of boiler feed water must include degasification. Removal of these gases such as oxygen and carbon-di-oxide, hydrogen sulphides etc. from water can be done by two processes-

- Gases which are removed by heating the solution, because solubility of gases in water decreases when the temperature is increased.
- Gases which can only be removed by chemical treatment. For instances, Oxygen from water may be removed by passing water over iron, as a result, iron is oxidized to ferric state and is precipitated.

$$4Fe + 3O_2 \longrightarrow 2Fe_2O_3$$

Acidic gases can be removed by treating water with calcium hydroxide or calcium carbonate resulting in a precipitate.

- In Ground water, there is no turbidity but contains more mineral salts such as free CO_2, Ca, Mg, iron and manganese salts etc. whereas surface water usually contains turbidity, Ca and Mg salts, silica, bacteria, various micro-organism, organic matter from sewage and industrial wastes. The temperature of groundwater is lower than that of surface water and remains almost constant.

1.1.4 Solubility of Gases in Water

The solubility of gases in water usually depends upon temperature and salinity of water. The solubility of gases decreases in water as a result of increase in temperature or salinity. CO_2 is about 200 times more soluble in water than oxygen. Oxygen dissolved in water is mostly utilized by living organism for respiration. The saturation concentration of oxygen in water is governed by temperature and salinity which makes oxygen a limiting factor for aquatic animals. The lower the temperature, the greater is the oxygen retaining capacity of water, no matter whether it is fresh water or sea water.

The amount of dissolved oxygen in water reduces due to respiration, decomposition of organic materials and stream pollution. In lakes and ocean areas the deepest layers of water usually have low oxygen concentration mainly because of continuous decomposition of organic materials (debris), respiration of organism and complete absence of photosynthetic activity. Oxygen is transferred to deeper water by diffusion or through circulation of water. Some aquatic animals such as crocodiles, whales, alligator, seal etc. obtained oxygen directly from the atmosphere, by coming on the surface of water reservoirs; therefore, these animals are totally independent of oxygen concentration in water.

Nitrogen is significantly less soluble in water than oxygen. Nitrogen is chemically inert and it does not react with water.

Carbon-di-oxide is produced by the decomposition of organic matter and also due to respiratory activity of aquatic plants and animals. CO_2 combines with water and form carbonic acid (H_2CO_3) which influences the pH or H^+ ion concentration of water. Carbonic acid being unstable compound, dissociates to produce H^+ ions and HCO_3^- ions. The bicarbonate ions may further dissociate to give more of H^+ ions and carbonate (CO_3^{2-}) ions.

$$CO_2 + H_2O \rightleftharpoons H_2CO_3 \rightleftharpoons H^+ + HCO_3^-$$

$$2H^+ + CO_3^{2-}$$

The amount of free CO_2 in water governs the precipitation of calcium in the form of $CaCO_3$. The precipitation of $CaCO_3$ occurs in presence of high temperature and high salinity and when amount of free or uncombined CO_2 is low. Such condition are usually found to exist in shallow tropical waters, where evaporation is high. Evaporation increases the salinity and photosynthetic activity of plants and thus reduces the amount of free CO_2 in water. In deeper layer of ocean, temperature are low and no photosynthetic activity takes place which eventually leads to higher content of carbon-di-oxide. Therefore, deep water fauna possess very fragile skeleton as the precipitation of $CaCO_3$ is minimum.

Natural water contains ions which are responsible for the salinity of the water. The salinity of fresh water varies from place to place. Salinity of marine water is about 3–3.5 percent. The salinity of various salts lakes varies from 25 percent to even 30 percent or more which greatly restricts life exist in them.

1.1.5 Water-Essential for Human

Water has physiological importance in human body and has specific function to perform which are as following–

- Being excellent solvent, it helps to regulate electrolyte balance of the body and maintains a healthy equilibrium of osmotic pressure excreted by solute dissolved in water.
- Water acts as a solvent for the secretory and excretory products and as a carrier of nutritive elements to tissues and it also helps to removes waste materials from them. Besides, it also acts as a regulator of body temperature.

1.1.6 Excellent Solvent: Water

The two most important properties of water which makes water an excellent solvent are:

- Water is a polar molecule and has a dipole moment
- Water has a high dielectric constant.

a) Water is a polar molecule because of which there is a force of attraction between any ions and water molecule which is of opposite sign. This attraction is referred as Ion-dipole force of attraction. The force of attraction between ions and the dipolar H_2O molecules causes the formation of hydrated ions that are lower in energy than the separated ion and water molecule.

The lattice energy is the amount of energy required to separate the crystal into gaseous ions. The hydration energy is the amount of energy released when isolated ions are hydrated. The heat of solution is the difference between lattice energy and the hydration energy. If heat of solution is positive, the process of dissolution is endothermic and heat needed to be supplied in order to dissolve the crystal at constant temperature.

For instance, Dissolution of NaCl, KI, NH_4NO_3, $Na_2CO_3.10H_2O$ etc. is endothermic. These compounds dissolve readily in water because of increase in molecular disorder on dissolution.

If heat of solution is negative, the process of dissolution is exothermic and heat is evolved as a result of dissolution of the crystal.

For instance, Dissolution of LiBr, NaOH, $CaCl_2$, Na_2SO_4 (anhydrous) is exothermic.

b) Water has high dielectric constant which makes it easier to separate ions in water in comparison to any other liquid with lower dielectric constant. Dielectric constant may be defined as the ratio of the work required to separate two oppositively charged particles a given distance in vacuum to the work required to separate them to the same distance when they are immersed in a liquid. The greater the dielectric constant of the medium, the smaller the force between charged particles. Most of the organic solvents have dielectric constant between 2 and 10. The dielectric constant of alcohols is in between 20 and 35. As per dielectric constant formula 'the work required to separate opposite charges a fixed distance is inversely proportional to the dielectric constant.

For instance, Work required in water/Work required in C_2H_5OH

$$= 24.30/78.54 = 0.309 = 30.9\ \%$$

This shows that it is much easier to separate the ions of an ionic crystalline solid in water than in alcohol. Therefore, water is much better solvent than ethanol for such solutes. A very few liquids such as anhydrous H_2SO_4 have dielectric constant greater (101.2) than water (80.54).

c) Dipole moment is a property of an individual molecule, but dielectric constant is a property of the liquid as a whole. Hydrogen bonding is also responsible for very high dielectric constant of water. Dipole moment of water and ethanol are almost similar, i.e. for water it is 1.85D and for ethanol it is 1.69D, but dielectric constant are quite different, being 80.54 and 24.30 respectively.

The higher the temperature of liquid water, the more hydrogen bonds are broken and the less order that exists. This means that dielectric constant of water decreases with increases in temperature.

For example, the dielectric constant of H_2O at 0 °C is 88.0;

$$at\ 25\ °C\ is\ 78.54$$

$$at\ 100\ °C\ is\ 53.3\ respectively.$$

Some hydrogen bonding still persists in H_2O even at its boiling point, 100 °C. Alcohol have large dielectric constants than other organic liquids is also because of hydrogen bonding in alcohols.

1.1.7 Main Characteristics of Water

The main quality characteristics of water can be understood by following parameters,

    1.1.7.1 Alkalinity

    1.1.7.2 Hardness

    1.1.7.3 Total Solids

    1.1.7.4 Oxidation

    1.1.7.5 Transparency

    1.1.7.6 Silica Content

1.1.7.1 Alkalinity

The total content of substance in water that causes an increased concentration of OH^- ions either upon dissociation or as a result of hydrolysis is called Alkalinity of water. The alkalinity of water is mainly because of HCO^{-3}, $HSiO^{-3}$, SiO_2^{-3} and sometimes of CO_2^{-3}. As a result of hydrolysis, the salt of some weak organic acid (*called as humates*) binds H^+ ions, thereby increasing the concentration of OH^- ions, eventually adding alkalinity to natural waters. The alkalinity may be regarded as-

  – Bicarbonate alkalinity (A_b)
  – Carbonate alkalinity (A_c)
  – Hydrate alkalinity (A_h),

The classification of these alkalinity is depending upon the presence of HCO^-_3, CO^{2-}_3, and OH^- anion in water respectively. The total alkalinity (A_T) of water is determined by the amount of acid neutralized together with a methyl orange indicator for water titration. The total alkalinity also includes other ions that react with acid, including humates.

1.1.7.2 Hardness

The total hardness (HT) is defined as the concentration of Ca and Mg cation expressed in mg equivalents per kg (mg-equiv/kg) or microgram equivalent per kg (µg-equiv/kg).

Broadly natural water can be categorized into:

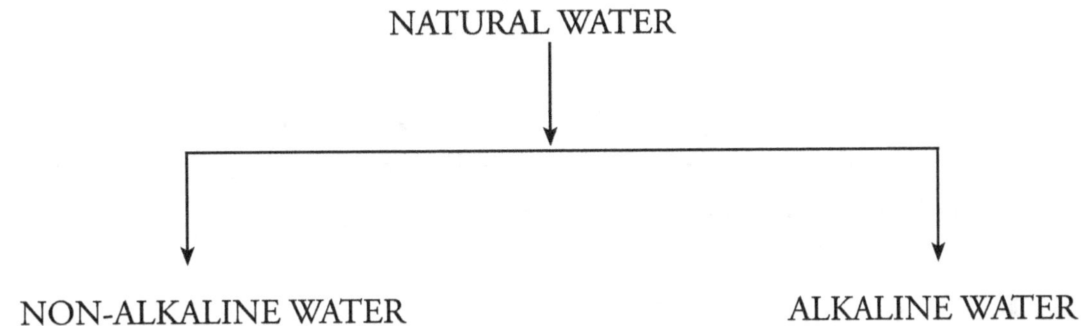

[These are characterized by the inequality $H_T > A_T$]   [These are characterized by the $H_T < A_T$]

The non-alkaline waters are characterized by the following types of hardness: Total Hardness (H_T), Carbonate Hardness (H_c), Non-carbonate hardness (H_{nc}), Calcium Hardness (H_{ca}), and Magnesium Hardness (H_{mg}). These hardness are related as: $H_T = H_c + H_{nc} = H_{ca} + H_{mg}$

Water which contains bicarbonates, sulphate, and chlorides of Ca and Mg are termed as hard waters. The water is referred as hard as it is hard to get lather with soap. [Soap is composed of sodium salt of higher fatty acids such as stearic, oleic, and palmitic acids]. The sample of water is called soft when it lathers readily with the soap. Hardness can broadly be categorized into temporary or carbonate hardness and permanent or non-carbonate hardness.

Carbonate or Temporary hardness is due to the presence of bicarbonate of Ca and Mg in water, which can be removed by boiling. The non-carbonate or permanent hardness is because of the presence of sulphate and chlorides of Ca and Mg and cannot be removed by boiling. Permanent hardness can be removed by utilizing chemical agents and other methods. Calcium hardness is a result of calcium compounds whereas magnesium hardness results from magnesium hardness. It should be noted that small amounts of salts and air dissolved in water give it the usual pleasant taste and presence of some portion of mineral constituents (necessary for growth of the body) makes hard water sometimes fit for drinking purposes. Hence, it is not always unfit for drinking purposes whereas soft water may contains impurities of an injurious nature which render it unfit for drinking. Therefore, soft water is not always fit for drinking purposes.

1.1.7.3 Total Solids

The amount of non-volatile substance present in water in a colloidal and a molecular dispersed state is referred as Total Solids. It is expressed in mg/kg. To determine the content of total solids in natural water, Ca and Mg bicarbonate are converted into carbonates, $CaCO_3$ and $MgCO_3$. Besides, there are three broad categories of total solids. These are,

- Fixed Residue Solids,
- Mineral Residue Solid,
- Sulphate Solid.

1.1.7.4 Oxidation

When water is contaminated by organic substances, it is usually characterized by oxidability. It is expressed in milligram of oxygen required to oxidize the organic compounds contained in 1 kg of water in given conditions. The oxidability is denoted as mg/kg O_2.

1.1.7.5 Transparency

Transparency reflects the pathways of light through the water. It depends upon the amount of substances or particles present in the water. The water transparency will be less if the content of particles present in water is in high quantity. The reason is that when particles are present in higher amount in water, the light cannot readily penetrate into the water column. Water transparency is measured by Sechhi disk as shown in Figure 1.1

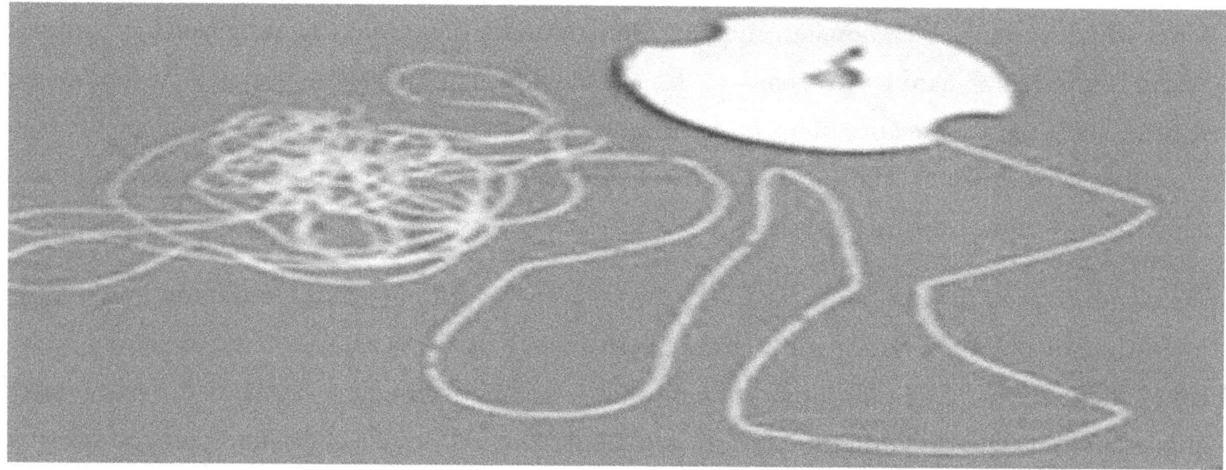

Figure 1.1 Sechhi Disk – Instrument to measure water transparency

(Source: http://www.rmbel.info/training/how-to-use-a-secchi-disk)

A Sechhi disk is basically a metal disk, 8 inches in diameter that is lowered into the water on a cord. The depth where secchi disk can no longer be seen through the water is referred as Secchi depth. When the transparency of water is high, the secchi depth is high, whereas when the transparency of water is low and cloudy, the secchi depth is low. Figure 1.2 depicts the use of secchi disk.

Figure 1.2 Use of Secchi disk for finding water transparency
(Source: http://www.rmbel.info/training/how-to-use-a-secchi-disk)

1.1.7.6 Silica Content

Silica is a compound of silicon and oxygen, referred generally as silicon dioxide (SiO_2). All natural waters supplies contain some amount of dissolved silica and mostly suspended or colloidal silica. The volcanic activity and the weathering process releases silicon into the water. Silica levels in water are usually reported as mg SiO_2/l. Silica in freshwater sources is found at concentration ranging from 1 to about 100 mg/l, with groundwater concentration typically at the higher end of that range.

1.2 Types and Sources of Water Pollution

The term 'Water Pollution' referred as any alteration in physical, chemical, and biological characteristics of water which may have adverse or detrimental effects on human and aquatic biota. Pollution is a general term, derived from the Latin word *pollutus* – Pol means before and Lutus means wash, and this also includes contamination. The Contamination is the explicit term used to indicate pollution. When it is referred that water is contaminated – it means that though water may not be objectionable to human senses of sight, odor, feel, and taste but water is totally unfit for the drinking, it is unsafe and unreliable for use. Therefore, contaminated water is not expected to be apparently objectionable. For instance, water seems to be clear on sight but on proper examination, is found to contain harmful pathogenic bacteria. Whereas, in comparison to contaminated water, polluted water is objectionable to the human senses of sight, odor, feel and taste. For instance, the water which appears to be colored, turbid, spreading offensive smelling, oily and greasy water and later on conducting chemical or physiological or biological examination, ensures that water is polluted.

1.2.1 Types of Water Pollution

Water pollution can be classified broadly into two categories-

1.2.1.1 On the basis of the physico-chemical analysis, it is classified into;

    a) Physical pollution of water
    b) Chemical pollution of water
    c) Biological or Bacteriological pollution of water

1.2.1.2 On the basis of sources and storages of water, it is classified into;

    a) Groundwater pollution
    b) Surface water pollution – Lake water pollution,
                      – River water pollution,
                       – Sea water pollution.

1.2.1.1 On the basis of Physico-chemical analysis-

a) Physical pollution of water –

The sources of physical pollution in water may be agricultural, domestic or industrial wastes. These wastes bring about changes in water with regard to its color, density, odor, taste, turbidity, and thermal properties etc. Few are mentioned below in detail-

Color – Water changes its color due to interaction between naturally occurring components in water and trade effluents that make it unsuitable for various purposes. Tannery wastes containing tannins when discharged into iron containing water streams, interacted with iron and changes color from deep green to blue.

Turbidity – Turbid water indicates high concentration of sewage or industrial effluents. Turbidity makes water unsuitable for industrial purposes as well as for domestic use because of various toxic metals such as Fe, Ni, Co, Pb, Bi, Mn etc, these may cause stains on cloths, sinks and baths etc. Turbidity measurements are useful to follow the course of self-purification of rivers and streams. Coagulants like ferric sulphate, ferric alum, ferric chloride etc. can be used to check turbidity of water. Turbidity in water arises mainly from colloidal matter, suspended particles. The suspended particles when presented in water can able to damage fisheries as it decreases the penetration of sunlight into the water. The presence of foam or froth in water indicates suspension of gas in water. Foam when persist for a long, indicates presence of chemicals, soap, detergents or certain industrial waste. The pollution of water due to the presence of foam is one of the serious pollution, as foams is likely to carry pathogenic bacteria also.

Taste – Water is tasteless, but the presence of pollutants such as Mn, oils, HC, pesticides, chlorophenols, petroleum products, oils and grease etc. produces characteristics taste in water. Besides the decomposed organic matter, fungi, bacteria, algae, pathogens etc. imparts peculiar taste.

Odor – Water is odorless, but the presence of chemical and biological agents such as certain organic and inorganic compounds of nitrogen, sulphur, phosphorous present in sewage causes foul odor in water. Whereas, microorganisms like oscillatoria causes muddy odor and algae, Anabaena produces a strong grassy odor. Protozoa imparts fishy odor to water. Royal Commission on Sewage Disposal, London identified the odor from polluted water as follows-

- Fishy odor due to organic amines,
- Rotten eggs/putrid smell due to hydrogen sulphides,
- Wormy smell due to phosphorous compounds,
- Earthy odor due to humus.

b) Chemical pollution of water –

The sources of chemical pollution of water are mainly dyes, drugs, insecticides, detergents, pesticides, and chemical industries, which releases inorganic and organic chemical such as acids, alkalis, toxic inorganic compounds, etc. The chemical pollution of water alters pH, dissolved oxygen, and other gases in water. The pollutants which are responsible for causing chemical pollution are organic or inorganic pollutants. The organic pollutants can be biodegradable or non-biodegradable. Biodegradable organic pollutants include Proteins from domestic sewage, waste from creameries, canneries, slaughter houses etc; Fats from sewage, soap production, wool processing; Carbohydrate, sugar, starch etc. from sewage, textile mills and paper mills. Non-Biodegradable organic pollutants are those which persist in the aquatic system for a very long time. *Take for instance* the pesticides, bactericides, herbicides, fungicides, insecticides, rodenticides, etc.

c) Biological pollution of water –

The sources of biological or bacteriological pollution of water are domestic sewage and industrial wastes. It is due to the presence of certain fungi, pathogenic bacteria, protozoa, viruses, parasitic worms etc. It is caused by the excretory products of warm blooded mammals such as man, wild, and domestic animals. The main pollutant belongs to the group of coliform bacteria, faecal streptococci and miscellaneous organisms. This water when consumed creates infections of the intestinal tract like cholera, dysentery, typhoid, gastroenteritis, polio, and infectious hepatitis.

1.2.1.2 On the basis of sources and storages of water-

    A)   Groundwater pollution
    B)   Surface water pollution a) Lake water pollution,
                                            b) River water pollution,
                                            c) Sea water pollution.

A) Groundwater pollution

Groundwater behaves as a reservoir due to the large pore space present in earth materials, as a channel which can transport water over long distances and as a mechanical filter which could improves water quality by removing suspended solids and bacterial contamination. Groundwater is the sources of water for wells and springs, that is eventually the source of rural domestic use. It is refilled by precipitation through rain, snow, sleet, and hail. It can be used approximately 416 cu km annually which would increase to 1108 cu km by 2025 AD. Groundwater contamination is generally irreversible, that is, once it is contaminated, it is difficult to restore the original water quality of the aquifer. Excessive mineralization of groundwater degrades water quality producing an objectionable taste, odor etc. Groundwater is a principle source of drinking water, particularly in rural areas and also for irrigation, but it has been extensively exploited and polluted that eventually damage agriculture as well as human health. The disposal of solid and liquid wastes containing heavy metals eventually leads to heavy metals contaminations of the soil-water-plant-animal ecosystem. There are several factors that affect groundwater pollution such as-

- Rain fall pattern,
- Distances from the source of contamination,
- Depth of water table,
- Soil properties such as texture, structure, and filtration rate.

Besides the important sources of ground water pollution is-

- Domestic wastes,
- Agricultural wastes,
- Industrial wastes,
- Soluble Effluents, and
- Runoff from urban areas.

Domestic and Industrial wastes – Domestic waste are responsible for deteriorating the water quality by releasing pathogenic organisms, nutrients, and solids. Industrial waste generally contains toxic heavy metals along with hazardous organic and inorganic effluents. The groundwater is fast getting polluted because of the impact of domestic and industrial wastes. *Agricultural wastes* – Wastes such as pesticides, fertilizers, insecticides, herbicides, processing wastes etc. are constantly added to water. Leachates of these wastes containing primarily nitrates, phosphates, potash, move downward with percolating water and join the aquifer below, posing danger to the groundwater. For instance, Methaemoglobinaemia or blue-baby diseases is mainly caused by the reaction of nitrate with haemoglobin, the oxygen carrier in the blood, producing methaemoglobin, which strangles the oxygen carrying capacity of the tissue. Besides nitrates is also responsible for eutrophication, other than phosphates.

Runoff from Urban areas and Soluble Effluents – River, lakes, and groundwater have been polluted by industrial effluents, pesticides, and fertilizers, from agricultural runoff and urban waste. Deforestation increases surface runoff and reduce groundwater. Almost two thirds of the world population by the year 2025 will be subject to moderate to high water management difficulties. Chronic water scarcity is common in areas where groundwater has been overdrawn from irrigation, industrial use or to meet the requirement of urban and rural population. Several soluble effluents pollute the ground water.

Harmful Effects of Groundwater Pollution-

- It is the major cause for the spread of epidemics and chronic diseases in man. It is responsible for typhoid, jaundice, dysentery, tuberculosis, diarrhea, and hepatitis.
- Severe groundwater pollution results from the presence of heavy metals such as iron, arsenic, fluoride, etc. Arsenic contaminated water causes black-foot diseases, melanosis, keratosis, skin cancer, etc.
- The use of polluted/contaminated ground water for irrigating agricultural fields severely damages crops and decreases grain production.
- Polluted or contaminated water increases alkalinity in the soils, affects soil fertility by killing bacteria and soil microorganisms. It also affects plant metabolism severely and disturbs the whole ecosystems.

The state government of Punjab has admitted that besides declining water level, the state is facing acute problem of water quality due to high concentration of arsenic and fluoride. It is reported by Department of water supply and sanitation, Punjab that at many pockets in the state the water is found to be completely unfit for human consumption. The areas of Patiala, Sangrur, and Fatehgarh Sahib are adversely affected with Fluoride while Amritsar, Tarn Taran belt are with arsenic. Nearly 700 habitations have arsenic beyond the permissible limit of 0.01 mg/l. As per March 2017 report, West Bengal groundwater is adversely affected with Arsenic in the country. It was noticed that 83 blocks in 8 districts of West Bengal have more than thrice the permissible limit of arsenic in groundwater. West Bengal government has provided safe drinking water to 52 percent of the arsenic-affected areas in West Bengal. Box 1.1 depicts key facts as of March 2017 regarding the status of groundwater in India.

Box 1.1 Key Facts

Key Facts, as of March 2017

- *The total number of people suffering from arsenicosis in India is about 1.48 crore.*
- *West Bengal is worst affected areas with more than 1.04 crore arsenicosis patient.*
- *Next to West Bengal is Bihar with 16.88 lakh people and next to Bihar is Assam with 14.48 lakh victims.*
- *According to World Health Organization guideline for drinking water quality, the permissible limit of arsenic is 0.01 mg/l (1993). EPA's adopted this guideline in 2004. However, in India, the guidelines are flexible. The areas or in some pockets where alternative are available, the permissible limit is 0.01 mg/l while where no other alternative is present, than permissible limit is 0.05 mg/l.*
- *West Bengal had initiated several projects to provide safe drinking water to more than 6 lakh people in the arsenic affected blocks. But, the expensive arsenic-treatment plants hampered the processes.*

B) Surface water pollution

Water has self-purification capacity. Before 1880, all the rivers were comparatively free from pollution. The emergence of industrial revolution encouraged the growth of factories which grossly polluted the surface water of river, lake, ponds, ocean, estuaries etc. The factors which affects surface water pollution are-

- Hydrological characteristics of diluting biocides and the extent of self-purification.
- Vegetation, soil type and degree of weathering rocks.
- Physical, chemical, and biological characteristics of effluents entering the surface waters.
- The functioning of treatment plants such as sewage or effluent treatment plants.
- Hygienic and health situation of the communities residing near surface waters. Besides the prominent sources of surface water pollution are – surface runoff, industrial and municipal waste, agricultural wastes, decomposed plant and animal matter, radioactive material.

United State Department of Health, Education and Welfare (HEW) has classified surface water pollutants into eight major categories. These are – Sewage and waste, infectious agents, particulate soils and mineral matter, dissolved toxic pollutants, mineral and chemical compounds, radioactive nuclides, thermal pollutants, and organic chemical exotics. The heavy load of pollutants decreases the rate of self-purification and it became more sensitive to propagation of life. There are various techniques available to purify water such as chelation, precipitation, coagulation, aggregation, oxidation, reduction, etc. which will discussed in detail in Chapter II onwards.

a) Lake Water Pollution

The prominent sources of pollutants in lake are the discharge of organic wastes from hills and toxic effluents from urban areas, industries. Box 1.2 depicts the states of lakes worldwide.

Box 1.2 Status of lakes

Status of Lakes

- World's largest lake – Salty Caspian Sea – Located between Europe and Asia (Kazakhstan, Russia, Azerbaijan, Turkistan, and Iran)
- World's largest floating lake – Loktak lake – Manipur, India
- World's largest fresh water lake – Lake Superior – North America
- World's deepest lake – Lake Baikal – Siberia
- Asia's largest fresh water lake – Manchar Pakistan
- Asia's biggest fresh water lake – Kolleru lake – Andhra Pradesh, India

The dysfunctional sewage and effluent treatment plants also releases toxic effluents in the lake water. Besides the surface runoff, rivulets, and streams from agricultural lands also enhance the situation of crises to disaster. Eventually these effluents cause eutrophication disrupting the whole aquatic environment. Table 1.2 depicts the status of pollution of lake in India.

Table 1.2: Status of pollution of lake in India

Name of lake	Place	Source	Result
Naini Lake	Nanital, U.P	Construction of building activity and tourist traffic	Fish died in the lake. Dissolved oxygen decreases below 2 ppm.
Ambazari Lake	Nagpur, Maharashtra	Release of industrial effluents into the lake	Once the only source of drinking water now is completely unfit for drinking purposes.
Powai Lake	Mumbai, Maharashtra	Rapid urbanization and industrialization	Hundreds of fish in the lake died because of the inflow of sewage water.

(Cont.)

Name of lake	Place	Source	Result
Pushkar Lake	Ajmer, Rajasthan	Discharge of municipal waste	Worst Polluted water reservoir
Deshalser lake	Bhuj, Gujarat	Garbage and sewage have been diverted to this lake	Worst polluted water reservoir
Kolleru Lake	Andhra Pradesh	Encroachment from landfills and indiscriminate fishing activities	Water is unfit from drinking purposes
Naraina Lake	Delhi	Pharmaceutical companies situated in and around Nariana	It is being systematically filled with garbage by local building contractors. Water is completely unfit for any activities.
Rewalsar Lake	Mandi, Himanchal Pradesh	Sewage flowing, siltation from the catchment area, vegetation was removed, and mushrooming of construction activities.	Water is totally unfit for drinking purposes.
Loktak Lake	Manipur	Construction of barrage	Water level in the lake is so rapidly declining that ultimately the Keibul National Park, may stop floating. It will soon be on the verge of extinction by the barrage.

Name of lake	Place	Source	Result
Ranmal Lake	Jamnagar, Gujarat	Urban effluents and hospital waste	Once the Paris of Saurashtra, now become the dump site for effluents. Toxic waste percolates down to the ground water level and contaminates groundwater also.
Dal Lake	Srinagar, Jammu and Kashmir	Discharge of untreated municipal waste	Chocked by the spread of aquatic plants and algae in it. Its area has shrunk from 33 square km to less than 10 square km in 50 years.

Eutrophication is generally referred as 'natural aging of lakes.' It is a natural process, derived from Greek word 'eutrophos' meaning well-nourished or enriched. C.H. Weber described eutrophication as nutrient rich conditions. The prominent source of eutrophication are fertilizer, domestic, and industrial waste, urban drainage, detergents, animal waste, and sediments. Broadly eutrophications are of two types – Natural and Cultural eutrophication.

Natural Eutrophication is the process of lake aging characterized by nutrient enrichment. During this process oligotrophic lake is converted into a eutrophic lake. It promotes the production of phytoplankton, algal blooms and aquatic vegetation including water hyacinth, aquatic weeds, water fern and water lettuce which in turn provides food for herbivorous zooplankton and fish.

Cultural Eutrophication is the same process which is speed up by human activities and eventually it adds 80 percent more nitrogen and 75 percent more phosphorous to lakes and streams. For example, Lake Mendota and Lake Washington witnessed rapid eutrophication due to man's activities. In India, Naini Lake, Dal Lake is undergoing rapid eutrophication as a result of sewage, domestic wastes, and detergent addition.

Effects of Eutrophication

- Algal bloom releases toxic chemicals which kill fish, birds, and other aquatic animals causing the water to sink.

- Decomposition of algal bloom reduces dissolved oxygen (DO) level in water. In an anaerobic condition, aquatic organism begins to die and leads to a stinking drain.
- In an anaerobic condition, some bacteria survive through reduction of nitrates. On complete exhaustion of nitrate, the last resort is reduction of sulphate yielding hydrogen sulphides causing foul smell and putrefied taste of water.
- These pathogenic microbes such as viruses, protozoa, bacteria etc. eventually results into spread of fatal water borne disease such as polio, diarrhea, typhoid, viral hepatitis, dysentery etc.
- Algae and other rooted weeds interfere with the hydroelectric power by clogging the filters, retarding the water flow, ultimately affecting water quality and water works.
- During eutrophication midge *Chironomous plumosus* and *Tubificid worms* develop extremely high populations creating anesthetic and economic problems in water bodies.
- The lake enduring eutrophication may become oxygen deficient destroying fish habitats eventually leading to the elimination of several desirable aquatic species in water.
- Prolonged eutrophic condition leads to dystrophic state. The lakes which receive huge amounts of organic matter from alloethonous source are called Dystrophic. Such lakes contain bog flora and humic acid in high amount while planktonic productivity is very low.

Control of Eutrophication

- To limit the nutrient value, the waste water must be treated before discharging into water streams.
- Eutrophication can be minimized by removing nitrogen and phosphorous at the source. Physico-chemical methods can be applied to remove dissolved nutrients.
- Algal blooms should be removed upon death and decomposition. The growth of these unwanted aquatic weeds can be checked by copper sulphate and sodium arsenite.

b) River Water Pollution

Due to increasing population, industrialization, urbanization, increasing living standards and broad spheres of human activities, water resources have been extensively exploited and eventually polluted. Major Indian River such as Yamuna, Tapti, Narmada, Ganga, Chambal, Daha, Damodar, Krishna, Cauvery, Mahi, Brahmaputra, and other rivers are severely polluted. Various laws were enacted to check pollutants and source of pollutants to control water pollution. River were severely polluted during the monsoon periods and minimum during the winter. The effects of effluent and discharge varies with the distance and nature. It was noticed that Damodar and Chambal River are extremely polluted up to more than 32 kms. Polluted water resources are mainly responsible for water borne diseases. According to WHO report nearly 900 million people are worst affected by diarrhea each year and an equal number suffered from diseases caused by roundworms.

One billion people worldwide still lack adequate supply of clean drinking water and nearly two billion people do not get water for proper sanitation. According to All India Institute of Medical Sciences (AIIMS) New Delhi, drinking water in South Delhi is severely polluted. In spite of using chlorine for disinfection, there are alarming prevalence of amoeba, parasites, bacteria, virus, and larvae of insects in drinking water, which are mainly responsible for causing water borne diseases as well as several eye and brain diseases. Various physical, chemical, and biological methods are available for purification of water. One such method is the use of *Moringa Oleifera* powder (a tropical tree), when mixed with water, the powder produces positively charged protein in the solution which then interact with the negative charges in the suspended organic and inorganic matter, thus through this process viruses are easily removed through settlement and filtration. According to the Ministry of environment and forest (MEF), most of the rivers in India are extremely polluted, mainly due to direct inflow of untreated sewage resulting in increase of BOD (Biological oxygen demand) and Suspended Solid and decrease of dissolved oxygen (DO) level. The Damodar River is the extremely polluted river carrying discharges from approximately 43 major industries. Yamuna, the river of life is now dying a slow death and normally referred as modern sewage. Daily it receives untreated domestic sewage, industrial effluents, fly ash, and other chemicals in Delhi alone. Gradually river has lost free flowing that has self-cleaning properties. Another factor that degenerate Yamuna River is the Eucalyptus tree grown along the river, which also draws large amount of water. To save rivers, Eucalyptus trees must be replaced by Neem (*Azadirachta indica*) or Keeker (*Acacia Karoo*) trees and ensure proper functioning of STP and ETP. Ganga, near Varanasi, U.P, India received highest pollution load due to the discharged of untreated sewage and industrial waste. Tanneries in Yanimbadi, Ambur, and Ranipet area of Tamil Nadu, India are discharging untreated effulents into the Polar River. Periyar, the river of life in Kerala, India is dying a slow death. Approximately 437000 tons of sand is being mined every day. Table 1.3 depicts the status of some of the important river polluted in India.

Table 1.3 Status of River Polluted in India.

Name of the River (In India)	Status
Ganga and Brahmaputra, North and East India	Indiscriminate use of gillnets are responsible for most of the death of aquatic animals especially dolphins. The Farrakka barrage has also restricted the movement of dolphins, thereby posing a serious threat to the species.
Polar, Tamil Nadu	Industries are discharging untreated effluents into the river.
Bagmati, Rajasthan	Highly polluted mainly due to filth.

(Cont.)

Bharalu, Assam	River has been reduced to a stagnant water body with high toxicity levels due to free CO_2 (FCO_2).
Thamraparni, Tamil Nadu	Major victim of brick kilns as a result river banks disappeared and paddy fields are worst affected.
Neyyar, Southern Kerala	Completely destroyed by merciless sand mining.
Pamba, also known as *Southern Ganga*, Kerala	Water table has extensively reduced due to sand mining.

The important reasons of killing of these rivers are – Sand mining, Deforestation, Brick Kilns, Pollution, and Salt water Ingress.

Sand mining – Sand is being mined persistently to supply sand for the construction eventually leading to the depletion of water tables, sinkage of riverbeds as well as drying up of wells. When sand is removed, the hydraulic gradient increases dangerously. This reduces the capacity of river water in recharging of ground water. It also increases salinity in the wells situated near the river.

Deforestation – Encroachments and settlements has ultimately resulted in deforestation. When a forest is cleared or depleted from the upper reaches of a river and sand is removed from the lower reaches, it finally leads to the death of a river.

Brick Kilns – Illicit brick kilns have destroyed the banks of rivers as well as paddy fields. As a result of brick kilns, riverbanks are disappearing ultimately shrinking to ponds of mud and stagnant water.

Pollution – Untreated disposal of waste of industries and domestic sewage are one of the prominent reason of river dying. Dsyfunctioning of effluent and sewage treatment plant are also responsible for the adverse impact on water reservoirs.

Salt water ingress – Sinkage of riverbeds causes saline water to enter up to 20–25 km during high tide summer. The major victims of salt water ingress are almost Kerala's entire river. According to WHO water containing more than 550 mg/l salinity is completely unfit for drinking.

c) Sea Water Pollution

Marine or sea water pollution is associated with the alteration in physical, chemical, and biological characteristics of the water. Water become thus unfit for human consumption as well as for industrial purposes. Chemically, sea water is a solution of 0.5 m NaCl and 0.005 m $MgSO_4$ containing traces of all conceivable matter in the universe. The prominent source of marine pollution are raw or untreated sewage, ship breakage, oil spills or oil leaks which resulted in increase in organic pollutants, chlorinated and hydrogenated hydrocarbons, heavy metals, polychlorinated biphenyl etc. Besides oil tanker collisions, accidents on shore installations also result in leaks. Oil and its product endanger the aquatic life in the surface layers as well as the coastal flora and fauna. Major sources of oil pollution in sea water are-

- Cargo tanker washings at sea,
- Import oil losses,
- Oily wastes from oil fields or refineries near the coast produces problems in coastal water,
- Oil spill when mixed with urban sewage, silts, plastics, pesticides, and toxic metals eventually complex the pollution problem in sea.

1.2.2 Sources of Water Pollution

The prominent sources of water pollution are sewage and domestic wastes, industrial effluents, and agricultural discharges.

Sewage and Domestic Waste-

Sewage and Domestic waste contributes to the growth of pathogenic bacteria, protozoa, fungi, viruses etc. *Vibriocholerae, Salmonella typhosa, Shigella dysenteriae* are few example. Such wastes mostly contain faeces, soapy waste, food materials, papers, small plastics, detergents, kitchen wastes etc. Detergents used as cleansing agents, derived from surfactants (10–30 percent), builder (15 percent) and other ingredients. The persistent surfactants like alkyl benzene sulphonate usually interfere with the waste treatment processes by stabilizing the smaller particles thereby reducing the activity of secondary water treatment process such as biological filter beds and activated sludge processes. Water which is usually contaminated with detergents fetches a huge sheet of foam. The visible foam when mixed with toxic waste generates toxic foams which makes water completely unfit for any purposes as well as is objectionable also. Sewage and domestic waste makes water reservoir a repository of pathogenic organisms eventually leading to various water borne diseases. It also impedes the self-regulatory capabilities of aquatic organisms as well as self-purifying capacity of water bodies. It is also accountable for eutrophication by increasing the content of nitrates and phosphates.

Industrial effluents-

The characteristics of industrial waste depend upon the industrial processes in which they originate. For example the pathogen *Anthrax bacilli* is found in tannery wastes. Characteristically it contributes to water borne diseases. Generally all wastes generated from industries when discharged into water bodies without proper treatments adversely affects aquatic ecosystem. It imparts color, turbidity, and foul odor eventually reducing the dissolved oxygen, increases biological oxygen demand, temperature thereby when consumed by human it adversely affects kidneys, liver, brain, lungs, and reproductive system. For instances, the case of Minamata poisoning occurred in Japan in 1958. This involves mercury poisoning which occurred due to inorganic mercury discharged with industrial effluents. Mercury is widely used in industries which generate paints, pulp and paper, electrical equipment, batteries, medicines, dental amalgams, mercury vapor lamps, domestic thermometer and pesticides. It was methylation of the mercury that adversely affects human populations. The industrial effluents containing methyl mercaptan, penta chloro phenol reduces the photosynthetic rate of aquatic communities by obstructing sunlight penetration into the water bodies. Effluents containing toxic metals such as arsenic, lead, cyanide, cadmium etc. discharged into water bodies without treatment, contaminate water reservoir and when consumed by human disrupts peripheral circulation, liver cirrhosis, hyperkeratosis, melanosis, black foot disease, cancer, growth retardation, and cellular degeneration in brain.

Agricultural Discharges-

Modern agricultural heavily depends on chemical fertilizer, pesticides, herbicides, insecticides etc. Though they support agriculture but they also disrupts entire natural aquatic ecosystem. Excessive use of fertilizer to the soil habitually leads to accumulation of nitrates and phosphates in surface water bodies. It also pollute groundwater and when such contaminated water is consumed by human it adversely affects health. For instance, nitrate poisoning causes Methaemoglobinaemia. Such nitrate poisoning is very common in Rajasthan, India. It is found that in Rajasthan, India nitrate presence at some pockets are more than the permissible limit of 45 mg/l by WHO. Excessive use of chemical fertilizer gradually depletes soil fertility as soil cannot support essential microbes, humus for long period. Agricultural discharges also increases nutrient content thus making water bodies eutrophic that is highly productive, and this phenomenon is referred as eutrophication.

1.3 Industrial Wastes

The points which are going to be covered in this section are as follows-

   1.3.1 Characteristics of Industrial wastes

   1.3.2 Types of Industrial wastes

   1.3.3 Principle of Industrial waste treatment

   1.3.4 Terminologies used in waste treatments.

1.3.1 Characteristics of Industrial wastes

Industrial waste differ from industries to industries. For instances, Paper and pulp industries wastes mostly contains carbohydrates, while wastes generated from tanneries, dairies, slaughter houses are rich in nitrogen, and also contains excessive amounts of pathogenic organism. Industries manufacturing detergents, plastics, explosives, pesticides, fertilizer mostly produces chemical and toxic wastes. Metal plating industries generates wastes that are extremely toxic as well as rich in metals like nickel, cyanide, hexavalent chromium, etc. Broadly it could be divided into three categories-

- Waste rich in suspended matter in solid form. For example, china clay works, coal washeries etc.
- Waste that contains polluting matter in solution as well as suspended solid matter. For example, tanneries, dairies etc.
- Wastes that contain polluting substances mostly in solution form. For example, electroplating industry.

Besides the variations in the characteristics of industrial wastes depends mostly on the nature of the industry by which it has been formed or developed. For example, Rubber factories wastes generates extremely foul odor that it can be detectable even at low concentration making water unpleasant due to this reason, rubber factories are strictly not allowed to discharge their wastes into water bodies or reservoirs.

1.3.2 Types of Industrial waste

Industrial waste can be broadly classified into two types-

- Process waste
- Chemical waste

** Process waste –*

The wastes generated during processing. Every industries generates its own characteristics process wastes as a result of various operations such as washing of product container, washing of raw materials, formation of intermediate as well as final products. The process wastes are generally of two types – Inorganic process and Organic process.

Inorganic process waste mostly generated from chemical manufacturing industries, metallurgical industries, petroleum industries, electroplating industries etc. These wastes are generally high in toxicity. When it is mixed with organic wastes, they cause difficult in the removal of organic wastes. *Organic process* includes the wastes mostly discharged from dairies, tanneries, food processing industries, breweries, distilleries, paper mills, organic chemicals manufacturing industries, textile etc. The prominent problem with such wastes lies in their disposal.

** Chemical waste –*

Industries manufacturing detergents, explosives, dyes, pesticides, fertilizer, plastics, acids, base, resins, etc. contain chemical wastes. Chemical processes differ extensively as per the nature of the substance needed to be manufactured. The chemical wastes discharged from industries manufacturing industries, TNT, silicones, smokeless powder are acidic in nature and mostly requires neutralization.

1.3.3 Principle of Industrial Waste Treatment-

There are various factors, on which the method of treatment of an industrial waste depends such as,

- Nature of Industrial waste,
- BOD and COD of the effluents,
- Suspended solid present,
- Pollutants present,
- Toxic chemical substances present,
- pH value of effluents, and
- Total solids presents.

For each and every particulate waste, different treatments are adopted based on the characteristics of wastes. For example, in pharmaceutical industry the characteristics of waste from factory generating novalgin differ from the characteristics of waste from any sulpha drug industry, thus the waste generated required different treatment process. Another example can be the wastes containing phosphorous. Such phosphorous containing waste are mostly treated with flocculating agents. Further the volume of such waste can also be reduced to minimize the effects on water reservoir by-

- Classifying the waste at source,
- Conserving the waste water,
- Changing production to decrease the wastes,
- Reducing batch discharge, and
- Reusing treated effluents for gardening or any other purposes except drinking.

In India all types of wastes are usually mixed in one pipelines and discharged, thus reducing the volume. For example, the waste from cooling are separated and discharged directly as waste water without any treatment or it can also be reused in the industry itself, while other waste are transferred for treatment. Thus this type of volume reduction is achieved by *classification of waste at source.*

Second method to reduce the volume of industrial waste is *conserving the waste water* that is using less water. Water cost and treatment cost can be saved and reduced if the water is recycled and treated after a number of cycles. The recycling of waste water means reducing the volume of industrial waste, and thus promoting the water conservation. For instance, paper mill usually releases approximately 180 m^3 to 340 m^3 of water per ton of paper produced depending on the supply of water. The supply of water is reduced during summer hence paper mill uses less water during summer without harming the production. Therefore, if paper mill practices the same water economy throughout the year, not alone in summer, and water used is recycled, the volume of industrial waste produced can be much reduced

Another method to reduce the volume of waste is either controlling or *changing the process or design of manufacture* to reduce the volume of waste. For instance, the electrolysis of sodium chloride in mercury cells produces sodium hydroxide and carbon dioxide. Mercury is also discharged with waste water and when mixed with water reservoir, it contaminate with mercury eventually causing mercury poisoning. If this is replaced with diaphragm cells, there is no danger of water contamination or pollution. Therefore, it would be much better to switch over from mercury cells to diaphragm cells to avoid contaminations of water.

Another method is to reduce the batch discharge. This can be reduced by-

- Increasing the frequency of the discharged so that the magnitude of batch discharge is reduced, and
- By holding the batch discharged in basins and allowing it to flow uniformly and continuously.

Besides reducing the volume of waste, it is also inevitable to reduce the strength of waste. The strength of waste can be reduced by various methods such as-

- *Changing the process and the quantity of raw materials,*
- *Modifying the equipment,*
- *Removing obsolete technologies and replacing it with new eco-friendly technologies,*
- *Equalization of waste,* means when strong wastes from the industries are discharged in batches, it often suddenly increases the characteristics of waste. This produces unnecessary harmful loads. Thus, it is inevitable to equalize the discharge by retaining up the water in retaining basins and discharging it gradually in batches. This process stabilizes the pH, BOD, COD, suspended heavy solids. Further, they can be easily treated using other treatment technologies. Equalization method sometimes also produces such effluents which do not require any further treatment and can be directly released into water reservoir.
- *Segregation of wastes,*
- *Recovery of by-products etc.*

1.3.4 Terminologies Used in Waste Treatment-

1. *Biological oxygen demand (BOD)* – The amount of oxygen used up during oxidation of oxygen demanding waste when sample of water is incubated at 20 °C for five days with dissolved oxygen measured before and after. Various factors can influence BOD test such as dilution rate,

nitrification, toxic substances, temperature of incubation, and nature of bacterial seed as well as presence of anaerobic organism.

2. *Chemical oxygen demand (COD)* – The quantity of oxygen required for complete oxidation of all reducing substances of organic as well as inorganic origin present in the water. The COD test uses the oxidizing agent potassium dichromate to oxide organic matter in the sample. The test is widely used because it takes less time approximately three hours comparative to other test such as the BOD_5 which takes five days. The COD test does not, nevertheless, differentiate between biodegradable and non-biodegradable organic matter.

3. *Total Suspended Solid (TSS)* – This is the sum of the organic and inorganic solid concentration and it can be further divided into – Suspended Solid, Organic Solid, Inorganic Solid, Settleable Solid, and Colloidal Suspended Solid. Dissolved solids generally refer to that fraction of solids that pass through a 0.45 µm filter paper.

4. *pH* – This is basically a concentration of hydrogen ion activity in solution and indicates the level of acidity and alkalinity of an aqueous solution. If the pH of waste water is found to be outside the range of 5–10, there may be considerable interference with biological processes.

5. *Total phosphorous* – This basically involves orthophosphate, polyphosphate, and organically bound phosphate. Total phosphorous analysis requires conversion of polyphosphate and organically bound phosphorous to dissolved orthophosphate. Dissolved orthophosphate is then determined using colorimeter.

6. *Total Nitrogen* – This refers to the sum of measurement of total oxidized nitrogen (nitrates and nitrite) and total kjeldahl nitrogen that is ammonia and organic nitrogen.

7. *BOD: Nitrogen: Phosphorous ratio (C: N: P)* – In order to activate sufficiently microorganism requires a balanced diet. This is commonly attained by sustaining the level of C: N: P in the waste water at about the ratio of 100:5:1.

8. *Biological treatment of waste water* – Bacteria are the most heavily populated of the microorganism used in waste water treatment. These organism directly break down the polluting matter in waste water. Saprophytic bacteria are harmless and feed upon dead organic matter while Pathogenic bacteria are those which causes diseases in man and animals. *Vibrio cholera* (causes cholera), *Salmonella typhi* (causes typhoid), and *Shigella dysenteriae* (causes bacillary dysentery).

9. *Batch Discharge* – When waste water is discharged at intervals, the volume and strength of waste is usually be high, and this process is referred as batch discharge.

10. *Sewage* – The liquid waste generated from the communities which has tremendously foul odor. It usually includes sullage, discharge from latrines, urinals etc., industrial waste and storm water. Storm water means water from terraces open yards after a rainfall also carries a good quantity of organic matter.

11. *Night Soil* – It is used to indicate human and animal excreta.

12. *Combined Sewage* – Combination of sanitary sewage and storm water with or without industrial waste.
13. *Domestic Sewage* – Also refers as sanitary sewage, basically liquid waste generated from residential and business buildings and institutions. It may or may not contain storm water.
14. *Crude or Raw Sewage* – The sewage that has not been treated.
15. *Industrial waste* – The liquid waste in which effluents are present as main wastes.
16. *Dilute or Weak Sewage* – The sewage containing less suspended solid matter.
17. *Sullage* – The liquid waste from kitchen, bathrooms, sinks etc. It does not create any foul or bad smell because it does not contain human or animal excreta.
18. Refuse – Dry rubbish from stretch and house sweepings. This basically includes garbage, storm water, sewage, subsoil and sullage.
19. Garbage – This includes all types of semi-solid and solid waste food and products such as decayed fruits, grass, leaves, plastic pieces, sweepings, waste meats etc.
20. Septic Sewage – This indicate sewage which is in process of treatment.
21. Sewerage – The system of pipes laid for carrying sewage.
22. Conduit – The general terminology used for a carrier of any shape to transmit any fluid.
23. *Sewer* – The underground conduits through which sewage is allowed to pass are known as sewer. It can be of various types such as-
    Combined sewer is the sewer that carries domestic sewage and storm water. *Common sewer is* the sewer on which all the inhabitants have equal legal rights.
    Intersepting sewer is the sewer that can intercept the discharge from a number of main or outfall sewers. This basically transmits the flow to the point of treatment and disposal.
    Lateral sewer – the sewer that attains its discharge directly from the buildings. This indicates the first stage of sewer collection.
    Main sewer is the sewer which attains its discharge from a few branch or sub main sewers.
    Outfall sewer is the length of main or trunk sewer between the connections of the lowest branch and final point of disposal.
    Relief sewer – It is also refers as overflow sewer. Basically it is the sewer that carries excess discharge from an existing sewer.
    Trunk sewer – the sewer which gets its discharge from two or more main sewers.
24. *Sludge* – The semi-liquid which is produced from the solids of the sewage, and get accumulated at the bottom of settling tank refers as sludge.

1.4 Heavy Metals and Water Pollution

Heavy metal referred to a group of metals and metalloid with a density of more than 5 g/cm^3 or 4000 kg/m^3 or five times more than water. It can be said that elements having atomic weight between 63.5 and 200.6 while specific gravity greater than 5.0 commonly referred as heavy metals.

Take for example, Sn, Pb, Fe, Hg, As, Ag, Hg, etc. Osmium is considered to be the heaviest metal with a density of 22.5 g/cm³ while Lithium is considered to be the lightest metal with a density of 0.53 g/cm³ (Light metals generally referred to those whose density is less 5 g/cm³).

Heavy metal generally occurs in the earth's crust and through natural processes, it get solublise in groundwater. This process is speed up by anthropogenic or artificial processes eventually contaminating the water reservoir. It causes serious adverse impact on human and animal health by accumulating especially in kidney and liver. Exposure to heavy metal poisoning is mainly occurred from drinking water and enters into the food chain. The mobility, toxicity, and reactivity of heavy metal depend on its speciation.

The most toxic forms of heavy metal in their ionic species are the most stable oxidation states. For example, Ag^+, As^{3+}, Pb^{2+}, Hg^{2+}, Cd^{2+}, etc. in which they are more reactive with the body's bio-molecules eventually forming stable bio-toxic compounds which are extremely difficult to separate.

Heavy metals pollution of waste water is one of the prominent environmental problems throughout the world. It adversely affects plants. The significances of heavy metal toxicity is the excessive gathering of –

- Reactive Oxygen Species (ROS), and
- Methyl glyoxal (MG).

Both of these (ROS and MG) are responsible for – peroxidation of lipids, oxidation of protein, inactivation of enzymes, DNA damages, and interact with other vital constituents and thus damage them.

Plants are exposed to heavy metal which can be broadly divided into two groups-

- Redox active (Cu, Fe, Co, Cr), and
- Redox inactive (Zn, Cd, Al, Ni).

The redox active heavy metals are involved directly in the redox reaction in cells while redox inactive also results in oxidative stress through indirect mechanism.

Another important mechanism of heavy metals toxicity is the capacity to bind strongly to oxygen, sulphur, and nitrogen atoms. Due to this heavy metal toxicity there is growth retardation in plants including necrosis, chlorosis, turgor loss, a crippled photosynthetic apparatus, a reduction in the rate of seed germination often associated with plant death. Various technologies are available to mitigate heavy metal pollution such as chemical precipitation, membrane filtration, ion-exchange adsorption, electrochemical treatment technologies etc. Table 1.4 depicts the sources, impact on health and important information associated with it. The possible available treatment is also depicted in Table 1.4.

Table 1.4 Sources, Impact of heavy metal on health.

Heavy Metal	Sources	Impact on Health	Treatment
Lead (Pb)	Coal, Automobile, Paper, Dyeing, and Petrochemical industries, Mining	Lead Poisoning also known as Plumbism mostly occurred among Cattle, Sheep, and Horses. Learning Disability and Mental Retardation. Encephalopathy, a disease of the brain in children.	Chelation, Low calcium, high phosphate diet is recommended be used to control it.
Chromium (Cr)	Tannery, Fertilizer, Textile, Photography industries, and thermal power plants, mining. Natural sources such as Volcanic emission, weathering of soil and rocks.	Bronchial, Asthma, Allergies. Hyperglycemia and depletion of liver glycogen liver, lactic acid, and LDH activity. Cr (VI) is more toxic as it is more mobile in comparison to Cr (III).	Electrochemical treatments
Cadmium (Cd)	Nuclear and Power plants, Coal, Batteries, Ceramic toys, Electronic Industries.	Disability and Painful skeleton deformities, Vomiting, Nausea, Headache. Itai Itai diseases (In Japenese, it means – It pains, It pains) or Brittle bone disease, or Ouch Ouch disease.	Common antidotes are some chelating agents. But this treatment also depletes the essential elements of the body.

(Cont.)

Heavy Metal	Sources	Impact on Health	Treatment
Mercury (Hg)	Paper and Pulp, Coal, Power Plants, Cement, Pesticides, Cosmetics industries, Mining.	Disorder of the nervous system, Minamata Disease or Cerebral palsy. Also known as Cat's dancing diseases or the strange disease in Japan, among the local people.	All chloro-alkali plants must stop using mercury electrodes and switch to new technology.
Copper (Cu)	Electrical wire, piping, utensils, domestic in industrial and agricultural discharges.	Cu poisoning causes several abnormalities in the behavior, respiration. Menkes Disease affects mostly infants occurred due to Cu deficiency. The toxic effects of Cu causes congestion of nasal mucous membrane and pharynx, metal fume fever, stuffiness of the head, diarrhea, jaundice, hypertension, etc.	Chelation agents are used. The metal bound to the chelating agents is then excreted through urine.
Vanadium (V)	Waste effluents from vanadium metal industries, alumina plants, textile mills, iron and steel industries.	Tongues get blue black and a blue line appears on the gums. Occupational health problems in industrial areas. Vomiting and Intensive Cough.	High doses of ascorbic acid or an intraperitoneal administration of 10 percent solution of calcium trisodium salt of diethylene triamine penta acetate.

Heavy Metal	Sources	Impact on Health	Treatment
Zinc (Zn)	Natural sources like weathering, erosion and other natural phenomenon. Anthropogenic sources like wood combustion, waste incineration, iron, steel, zinc production, municipal waste water.	Skin disease, gastroenteritis problem. Illness arising from the ingestion of acidic foods prepared in zinc galvanized containers.	Chelating agents are used.
Arsenic (As)	Natural sources such as weathering of sedimentary rocks, volcanic eruption, geothermal areas, and fossil fuels. Anthropogenic sources such as mining, metal refining process, burning of fossil fuels, etc.	Black foot disease. Melanosis (Hyperpigmentation and Hypopigmentation), Keratosis with or without anemia, Skin cancer, etc. One of the most alarming fact about arsenic poisoning is that the symptoms appears after one to five years and once it's, appear it's too late to cure the problem.	No specific treatment is available. Generally Chelating agents are used. The best possible way is to stop drinking arsenic contaminated water.

The prominent source of heavy metal is drinking water, cereals, pulses, vegetables, milk, fish, meat, etc. Besides toys, color, cigarettes are also the prominent sources. The disposal of untreated industrial wastes as well as domestic effluents contaminants the water reservoir with toxic heavy metal. The cation of metals like lead, arsenic, silver, barium, etc. even if present in trace amounts causes various toxic effects. Such toxic metals poisoning is commonly referred as Trace Metal Poisoning (TMP).

1.5 Thermal Pollution

Thermal pollution is well explained by Owen in 1985 – "The warming up of an aquatic ecosystem to the point where desirable organisms are adversely affected." The prominent sources of thermal pollution are-

- Nuclear power plants,
- Coal fired power plants,
- Industrial Effluents,
- Domestic Sewage,
- Hydroelectric power.

Nuclear power plants along with hospitals, research laboratory or institutions, nuclear experiments and explosions released a lot of unutilized heat and traces of toxic radionuclides into water reservoir. This increases the temperature of the water bodies eventually altering the aquatic ecosystem.

Coal fired power plants – Thermal power plants usually utilize coal as fuel. Their condenser coils are cooled with water from nearby lake or river release the hot water back to the stream thereby increasing the temperature the temperature to about 15 ºC.

Industrial Effluent – Industries manufacturing electricity like coal powered and nuclear powered plants require huge amount of cooling water for heat removal. While textile, paper and pulp, sugar requires cooling water in comparatively less quantity. Thus industries releases or discharges hot water according to their use, but eventually the end result is that they increase the temperature of water reservoir to an extent that dissolved oxygen level falls affecting aquatic organism.

Domestic Sewage – The domestic effluents which are discharged into the water reservoir without any treatment, they generally have higher temperature than the receiving water. This untreated sewage not only raises the streams temperature to a measurable extent but also creates numerous deleterious effects on aquatic biota.

Hydroelectric power – Generation of hydroelectric power, sometimes result is negative thermal loading in water system. This eventually increases temperature and decrease dissolved oxygen in water reservoir and thus affecting aquatic ecosystem.

As it is clear from above section that thermal pollution has adverse impact on aquatic organism. Some of the harmful effects of thermal pollution are-

- Reduction in dissolved oxygen,
- Direct fish mortality,
- Changes in water properties,
- Increases in toxicity,
- Interference with biological activities,

- Interference with reproduction,
- Variation in reproductive rate,
- Changes in metabolic rate,
- Increased vulnerability to diseases,
- Invasion of destructive organism,
- Destruction of organism in cold water,
- Undesirable changes in Algae population,
- Disruption of food chain,
- Increasing the demand of oxygen,
- Affecting longevity of aquatic organism by shorten its life,
- Affecting distribution of organism,
- Food shortage for fish,
- Affecting the physiology, metabolism, growth, and development of marine animals,
- Deleterious effects on bacterial growth by coagulation of their body cell proteins, melting of cell fats, reduction in the permeability of cell membrane and by increasing degradation rates.

1.6 Water Microbiology

Water is an excellent medium for the growth and proliferation of microorganism. The microorganism of water is mainly governed by climatic or physical, chemical, and biological condition of water. Both saprophytic and pathogenic microorganism are found in water which falls under the varied groups of bacteria, algae, fungi, protozoa, viruses, nematodes, etc. Wastewater generally contains microorganism which influence the activities of microorganism already present in the receiving water reservoir. As a result, these pathogenic microorganism contaminants the water reservoirs, that ultimately affects the health of human and other animal life.

Naturally microorganism of varied types is present at different stages of hydrologic cyclic process – in surface water, groundwater, and atmospheric water. Depending on the nature of specific aquatic habitats, different species of microbes are regarded as indigenous to specific habitats. Surface water is found to be highly contaminated with microbes due to human activities while ground water, bacteriologically produces water of good quality if precautions are manufactured to avoid contamination.

Organic pollutants are the prominent reason for the growth of saprophytic bacteria and fungi. The eutrophic lakes supports flourishing growth of bacteria and algae. The microorganism growing in lakes are the genera *Microcystis, Anabaena, Spirulina, Protozoa, Nostoc, Oscillatoria, Diatoms, Oedogonium* etc. Excessive growth of algae, sometimes at optimum condition bloom well and referred as water blooms and the phenomenon is known as Water blooming. Besides people suffering from communicable diseases also discharge pathogenic microbes in water reservoir through their excreta. Further, unhygienic environment at public places of water collection also exaggerate the problem. The majority of bacteria found in water belong to groups:

- Coliform group *(E. Coli, and Aerobacter)*,
- Chromogenic rods *(Xanthomonas)*,
- Fluorescent bacteria *(Pseudomonas and Alginomonas)*,
- Proteus group,
- Non spore forming rods, and
- Spore forming of the genus *Bacillus*.

E. Coli *(Escherichia Coli)* presence in water indicates the degree of water pollution. E. coli bacteria are found in the intestine of man and animals. These are harmless to man but their presence indicates water is polluted with human and animal excrements, and also indicates the presence of pathogenic microorganism which are responsible for dysentery, cholera, typhoid fever, diarrhea, polio, and other serious gastroenteritis and grave disease. The water is severely polluted if it contains more than 10000 E. coli bacteria per liter. The water quality is considered to be satisfactory if it contains 10 bacteria per liter, and can be used for drinking if it contains three or less than three bacteria per liter. The degree of pollution is designated by E. Coli index, which will be discussed in detail in next section.

1.7 Water Analysis and Analytical Methods

Analysis of water pollutants is inevitable to assess the water quality in order to provide pure water for drinking, domestic and industrial purposes. Besides, to trace the origin and extent of pollution in order to suggest a viable mitigation methods. In water analysis, the key factors which are used for completion of analytical methods are depicted in Box 1.3.

Box 1.3 Water Analysis – Key Factors

Water Analysis – The Key Factors

- Sampling,
- Selection of Parameters accordingly,
- Meticulousness and accuracy of method selected,
- Preservation,
- Reporting, and
- Proper Labelling.

Water analysis is generally expressed in milligrams per litre and in parts per million, where

$$1 \text{ ppm} = \frac{\text{One part of hardness}}{10^6 \text{ parts of water}}$$

Parts per million (ppm) means the number of parts of substances per million parts of water. This is also referred as milligram per liter (mg/l), therefore,

$$1 \text{ ppm} = 1 \text{ mg}/\text{L} = \frac{1}{1} \text{ million} = 0.000001$$

Another unit which is generally used is microgram per liter, also known as Parts per billion (ppb). It is basically the number of unit of mass of a contaminant per 1000 million units of total mass. Therefore, one ppb is one part in one billion.

$$1\text{ppb} = 1 \text{ } \mu g/\text{L} = \frac{1}{1} \text{ billion} = 0.000000001$$

A microgram per liter is one thousandth of a milligram per liter.

Therefore, 1 ppm = 1000 ppb

The number of parts per million (X_{ppm}) is equal to the number of parts per billion (X_{ppb}) divided by 1000;

$$X_{ppm} = \frac{X_{ppb}}{1000}$$

$$\text{For instance, } 0.01 \text{ ppm} = 10 \text{ ppb or } \frac{10_{ppb}}{1000} = 0.01 \text{ ppm}$$

Table 1.5 indicates the conversion of ppm to ppb.

Parts per million (ppm) or mg/L	Parts per billion (ppb) or µg/L
0.001	1
0.01	10
0.1	100
1	1000
10	10000
100	100000
1000	1000000
10000	10000000

There are varied parameters which are analyzed for determining water quality which are as follows;

1. Physical parameters,

    This includes determination of Temperature, pH, Color, Conductivity, Odor, Turbidity, Total dissolved Substances.

2. Inorganic or Chemical Parameters,

    This includes Hardness, Calcium, Magnesium, Chloride, Sulphate, Fluoride, Alkalinity, Nitrate, and Phosphate.

3. Toxic Metals parameters,

    This includes analysis of Arsenic, Lead, Zinc, Chromium, Cadmium, Mercury, Iron, Manganese, Copper etc.

4. Organic, Nutrient Demand parameter,

    This includes analysis of BOD, COD, DO, Phenols, Pesticides, Nitrate, Oil and Greece etc.

5. Bacteriological Examination

    This includes examination of Total Coliform and Most Probable Number (MPN). In this, bacteriological examination will only be discussed in detail.

6. Biological Examination,

    This includes the examination of Phytoplankton and Zooplankton.

7. Radioactive Elements Examination,

    This includes the examination of Alpha emitter and Beta emitter.

1.7.1 Bacteriological Examination

Bacteriological examination includes two important examination

a) Total Coliform Test , and
b) Most Probable Number.

a) Total Coliform Test

This examination involves Total Count Test and Coliform or E. Coli Test.

- Total Count Test

    In this examination, the sample of water with agar added to it, is placed in an incubator at 20° C for two days that is for forty eight hours or at 37° C for one day that is for twenty four hours. The bacteria in water grows and form colonies which can be seen and counted. For potable water, the total count should not be greater than 100 per milliliter of water.

- Coliform or E. Coli Test

    In this examination, it has been noticed that coliform in lactose medium undergo fermentation at 37 °C within two days or forty eight hours with the formation of gas. E.

Coli test is performed in three stages – Presumptive test, Confirmed Test, and Completed Test.

Presumptive Test – In this examination, the sample of water are kept in sterile tubes and lactose is added. The tubes are placed in an incubator for twenty four hours at 37 °C. If the gas is evolved, the test is positive and indicates the presence of bacteria. If no gas is evolved, the process is again examined at the end of fort eight hours. If still no gas is formed, the test is negative and no bacteria is present in a sample.

Confirmed Test – When a sample of water is found to be positive in the presumptive test, a small amount of lactose broth is transferred to another fermentation tube containing green lactose bite. If gas is formed, even after forty eight hours, the test is positive and indicates that water is unfit for drinking. Another method is in which a small portion of sample of water is taken on a plate containing endo – or eosin – methylene – blue – agar. The plates are kept at 37 °C for forty eight hours. The result is positive, if colonies are seen. A completed test is then carried out in order to establish the presence of E. Coli group of bacteria.

Completed Test – This examination is performed by adding the water sample to lactose broth fermentation tubes and agar tubes. The tubes are placed in an incubator for twenty four to forty eight hours at 37 °C. The result is considered to be positive and water is unfit for drinking, if gas is formed even after forty eight hours. If the test is negative, water is safe for drinking. Further examinations are only conducted to determine the type of bacteria present in water.

E. Coli Index – The approximate number or E. coli present in 1 milliliter of the water sample is indicated by E. coli index. The index must be less than three in case of potable water and it should not be greater than ten. Heavily polluted sample of water contains more than 10,000 E. Coli bacteria per liter. Slightly polluted sample of water contains 100 E. Coli bacteria per liter.

b) Most Probable Number (MPN)

When maximum number of examination are performed on a sample of water, the values obtained in most cases give the bacterial density which may be regarded as the bacteria content that is most likely to be present in water. This is referred as Most Probable Number (MPN). The MPN was initially computed by Hoskins in 1934 to evaluate coli-aerogenes tests by fermentation tube method. Table 1.6 is based on the all-purpose formula of Hoskin (1934) for computing the numbers of coliform existing in 100 mL of water and extracted from Dubey and Maheshwari, 1999.

Table 1.6 MPN of Coliform organism existing in 100 mL of water (*Source: Dubey & Maheshwari, 1999*).

Number of Positive Lactose Broth Tubes			Number of Coliform Organism	Number of Positive Lactose Broth Tubes			Number of Coliform Organisms
10 mL	1 mL	0.1 mL		10 mL	1 mL	0.1 mL	
0	0	0	0	3	0	0	8.8
0	1	0	2	3	0	1	11
0	1	1	4	3	1	0	12
1	0	0	2.2	4	0	0	15
1	0	1	4	4	0	1	20
1	1	0	4.4	4	1	0	21
2	0	0	5	5	0	0	38

The Most probable number is considered to be zero, if on examination all the portion of sample are found to be negative. If only one value is positive then the value is 2.2 per 100 mL and so on, taken from a standard MPN table.

The MPN is found to be more accurate in comparison to the Coliform Test. The reason is that the MPN is based on the statistical laws to the results of a number of test. It is the simplest and most popular method of measuring coliform.

As per the standard prescribed by WHO the coliform bacteria should not detected or the MPN index of E. Coli microorganism should be less than 1.0 in 90 percent of the samples tested throughout the year.

CHAPTER II

Water Treatment Process

"One Drop of Water is even precious so better treat it for the safety of the future"

– Dr. Anamika Srivastava

2.1 Introduction

Water is an excellent medium of pathogenic microorganism and responsible for various water borne diseases. Drinking water must be free from pathogens, toxic elements, and excessive amount of minerals, organic matter. Water supply structures started initially with the selection of source of water, after selection the next stage is to convert intake work to collect it, and then carry up to treatment plants. After water treatment, it is preserved or stored in clean water reservoir, from where it will be distributed to all public or consumers. Box 2.1 depicts the water supply structure.

Box 2.1 Water Supply Structure

Water Supply Structure

1. **Selection of source of water, which must be permanent, reliable and must have minimum impurities. These can be-**
   a) Surface water – * Streams,
      * Lakes,
      * River,
      * Pond, and
      * Impounded Reservoir.
   b) Groundwater sources – * Spring,
      * Infiltration galleries,
      * Wells – *Artesian well, Open or Dug or Open well, Tubewell*
      * Infiltration well.

2. **Construct Intake works**

   The main function of the intake work is to collect the water from the selected source and then discharge water by means of pumps or directly to the water treatment plants. Broadly intake works are further divided into four types-

   - Lake Intake,
   - Reservoir Intake,
   - River Intake,
   - Canal Intake.

3. **Conveyance of water**

   The next stage is to carry water to the treatment plants or places and this can be carried out in two ways-

   - If the source of water is at higher elevation than the treatment plant, the water can easily flow under gravitational force – *Open Channel, Adequate, and Pipe lines.*
   - If the source of water is at lower elevation then the treatment plant, then water can be conveyed by means of *Closed pipes* (Under pressure).

4. **Treatment plants**

   The treatment plants are selected based on the impurities in water as well as the quality of water required by the consumers. This means whether the treated water is supply for drinking purpose or recreational activities or it is to discharge back into the water reservoir as in the case of sewage or industrial effluents treatments.

   - Plain Sedimentation,
   - Sedimentation with coagulation,
   - Filtration,
   - Disinfection,
   - Water Softening,
   - Miscellaneous Unit.

5. **Distribution System**

   The distribution system ensures that water must reach to each and every consumers with required rate of flow. Depending upon the method, this includes broadly three ways-

   - Gravity System,
   - Pumping System,
   - Dual System (Also known as *Combined Gravity and Pumping System*).

6. **Layout of Distribution System**

   On the basis of layout as well as direction of supply, they are classified as follows,

   - Dead End or Tree System,
   - Grid Iron System,
   - Circular or Ring System,
   - Radial System.

7. **District Water Mains**
8. **Branches and Service Pipe**
9. **Consumers**
10. **Waste Water**

    From consumer, after several uses of water, they generate waste water which is then again subject to treatment process.

The traditional way to purify water used in India about 2000 B.C was to keep drinking water to copper vessels. Expose it to sunlight and after sometimes of exposure, filter it using charcoal. Second way is to boil the contaminated water and then exposed to sunlight. Afterwards a piece of hot water dipped in it several times and finally filters it through coarse clean sand. It was reported by Birdie and Birdie (2012) that the work of sanitation were assigned to the local bodies during British rule in India. But this was not progressed much due to lack of technical staff. The Bhore Committee for the first time identified the significance of safe water supply and sanitation in National Development Plan. After independence, in India for the first time the provision of water supply and sanitation in the states were made in the Community and Local Development works through first five year plan (1951–1956).

In this Chapter, the following points will be discussed in detail-

- Layout for Treatment plants,
- Industrial Waste Water Treatment,
- Purification of Water,
- Water supply in Rural Areas, and
- Water supply in Urban Areas.

2.2 Layout for Treatment Plants

The perseverance of waste water treatment is to eliminate the contaminants from water so that the treated water can meet the acceptable quality standards. Table 2.1 depicts water quality standard. The quality standard usually depends upon whether water will be reused or will be discharged into a water reservoir. Waste water which can be reused include discharge from – *Industries, Irrigation, and Municipalities.*

Table 2.1 Water Quality Standard

Parameters	Maximum Permissible limit
Physical Parameters – Color	15–25 (on cobalt scale)
Turbidity	5–10 (on silica scale)
Temperature	10 °–15 °C
Taste and Odor	Nil
Biological – MPN of Coliform Bacteria	Less than 1.0 in 90 percent of the samples tested throughout the year.
E. Coli	Less than 3
Chemical or Inorganic Parameters –	
pH value	6.6 to 8.00
Total Suspended and Dissolved Solids	500–1000
Hardness	75–115 CaCO3 equivalent
Barium	1 ppm
Arsenic	0.01 ppm
Cadmium	0.01 ppm
Chromium	0.05 ppm
Selenium	0.05 ppm
Manganese	0.05 ppm
Iron	0.30 ppm
Lead	0.05 to 0.10 ppm
Copper	1.04 to 3.00 ppm
Zinc	15.0 ppm
Silver	0.05 ppm
Fluoride	1.50 ppm
Cyanide	0.20 ppm
Phenolic substance	0.001 ppm (as phenol)
Sulphate	250 ppm
Nitrate	45 ppm
Chloride	250 ppm
Radiological Parameter – Alpha emitter	1μμc/L
Beta emitter	10μμc/L

The waste water treatment processes are generally grouped according to the water quality they are expected to produce. Figure 2.1 indicates the flow chart of all steps involved in waste water treatment. These process are usually grouped as,

a) Primary Treatment or Mechanical Treatment,
b) Secondary Treatment or Advanced biological Treatment, and
c) Tertiary Treatment or Advanced biological, chemical or physical treatment.

a) Primary Treatment –

It is also known as Mechanical Treatment. The removal of Settleable solids is called Primary treatment. In fact it includes *pretreatment, sedimentation and flotation.* It was reported by American Chemical Society (ACS) that primary treatments have the ability to reduce approximately sixty percent of total suspended solid, thirty five percent biological oxygen demand (BOD), thirty percent chemical oxygen demand (COD), twenty percent total nitrogen and approximately ten percent of the total phosphorous.

- *Pretreatment-*

Wastewater is pretreated to eliminate large floating and suspended solids which could inhibit with the normal operation of the succeeding treatment process. The pre-treatment operation may also embrace flow measurement and sometimes pre chlorination to prevent any odor that may originate during succeeding processes. It consists of screening and grit removal. This whole process is divided into – Manual and Mechanical Racked bar screen.

The materials that are removed by screening are usually incinerated.

Fixed Bar Screen – These are the most common type of screen used in domestic waste water treatment facilities. Bar screen are made up of parallel metal bars and have apertures in the ranges 20–60 nm for coarse screens and 10–20 nm for fine and medium screens.

Grit Chambers – These are provided to safeguard pumps from abrasion or scratch and to diminish the formation of heavy deposits in pipes and channels. Grit Chamber are usually designed as long chambers and the velocity of waste flow is reduced to 30 cm/sec, which allows settling of the grit material. The grit can be removed by scrappers.

Comminutor – The comminutor grinds large solids which can then be satisfactorily handled in the sedimentation tank.

Figure 2.1 depicts the flow chart of waste water treatment process.

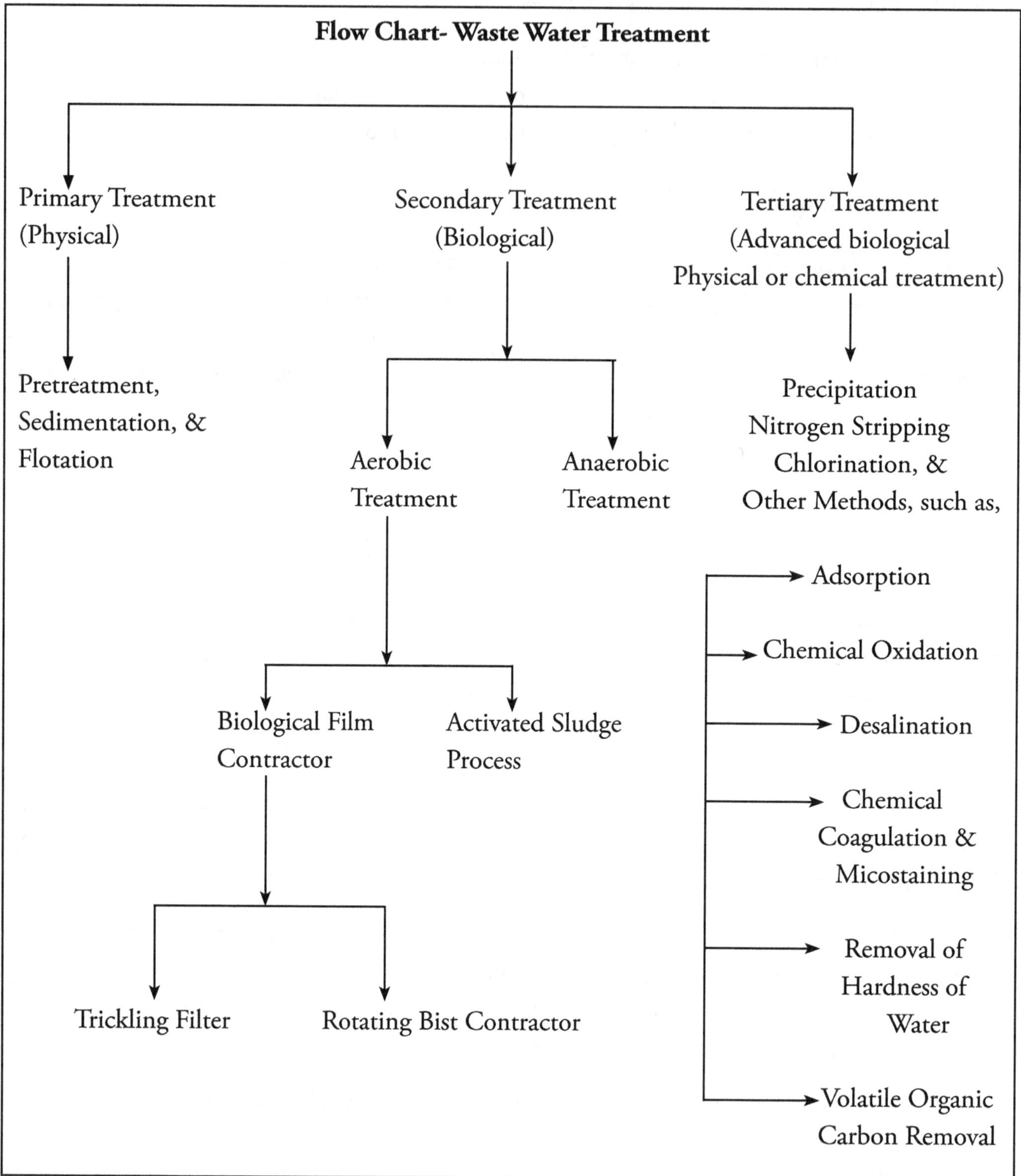

Figure 2.1 Flow Chart – Waste Water Treatment

- ***Sedimentation***

In this step, the settleable solids are detached by gravitational settling under quiescent or dormant conditions. The sludge formed at the bottom of the tank is removed as underflow either by vacuum suction or by racking it to a discharge point at the bottom of the tank for withdrawal. The clear liquid produce is known as the overflow, and it should contain no readily settleable matter. The sedimentation operation in waste treatment applications may be carried out in flow basins. The flow basin are broadly are of three types-

    i.   Rectangular Horizontal flow,
   ii.   Circular Radial flow, and
  iii.   Vertical flow.

Rectangular Horizontal flow – In this flow basin, the feed is introduced at one end along the width of the tank and the overflow is collected at the surface, either across the other end or at different points along the length of the tank. An endless conveyor scrapes the floating material into a screen though while it also pushes the settled solids into a sludge hopper.

Circular Radial flow – In this flow basin, the feed is introduced through a center well and the clarified effluents are collected at weirs along the periphery of the tank. Sludge removal is effected by means of a rotatory sludge scrapper who forces the settled sludge down a slopping bottom into a central hopper, from which it is withdrawn. Scum is removed by a surface skimming board which is attached to the rotatory mechanism and positioned in such a manner that the scum can be collected into a trough situated at the surface.

Vertical flow – They are often used in small treatment plants where the feed is applied at the point or points along the bottom, and clarifies effluent is collected at the top. A sludge blanket is maintained in the lower part of the tank through which the suspension rises. It is significant to control the sludge extraction and drain carefully to avoid losing the blanket, which acts as a filter for small particles.

Basic theory of Sedimentation

The settling of particles in a suspension depends upon their concentration and their flocculating properties. Generally there are three types of settling are recognized:

- Discrete Settling,
- Flocculent Settling, and
- Zone Settling.

Discrete Settling – The basic theory of sedimentation assumes discrete settling. Sedimentation of a particle from such suspensions is unhindered by the presence of other settling particles and is a function only of the properties of the fluid and the particle in question. When such a particle is positioned in a liquid of lower density, it will increase speed until a regulating terminal velocity is reached.

The terminal settling velocity (V_s) for spherical particles can be calculated using,

Q = Inflow Rate,

W = Width Tank,

H = Depth of Tank,

A = Surface Area of the Tank, and

V_s = Terminal Velocity of Particle depends on Viscosity or Density.

Therefore,

$$Q = \frac{H}{V_s},$$

$$V_s = \frac{Q}{WH} \qquad \text{Since WH = A,}$$

Therefore,

$$V_s = \frac{Q}{A}$$

By increasing the value of Q, V_s will be increase.

Flocculent Settling – This types of occurrence is clearly perceived in the Primary Clarifiers. The opportunity for amalgamation increase with the increase in bed depth, and as a result of the particle elimination efficiency depends on both the overflow and the bed depth. No reasonable origination is available for evaluating the flocculation consequence on the sedimentation. A settling column examination is usually accomplished by employing the test suspension in a column that has the equivalent depth as that of the sedimentation tank in question.

Zone Settling – This type of settling tank takes place in the Secondary Clarifiers of the activated sludge process, where the suspension is dense and the particles are so noticeably spread out that the velocity fields of the fluid displaced by the adjacent particles throughout settling overlap. There is an ascending displacement of the fluid with a lessening in the settling velocities of the particles, and this consequence is acknowledged as *Hindered Setting*.

The most frequently encountered form of *Hindered settling* occurs at very high particles concentration, where the suspension inclines to settle down with divergent interface between the settling solid and the clear liquid above it. This is characterized as *Zone Settling*.

- ***Floatation***

Floatation may be applied in place of sedimentation primarily for treating industrial waste water encompassing magnificently distributed suspended solid and oily matter.

Flotation technique is applied in paper industry to recover fine fibers from the screened effluent, and in the oil industry for the clarification of oil bearing waste. It is also applied for handling discharges from cold rolling, tannery industries, pharmaceutical industries and metal finishing.

A progressively significant production is the coagulating of the sludge acquired from activated sludge process. The particles of density precisely close to that of water are very problematic to settle in normal sedimentation tanks, and take a lengthy time for separation. For this reason floatation can be a better option where the separation can be exaggerated by aerating the discharge whereby air bubbles are attached to the suspended matter. This has the consequence of cumulative the buoyancy of the particles in the tank so that the air gets dissolved in the liquid. This is also known as the total pressurization or once through system.

The coagulants such as Aluminum sulphate, also known as alum can be applied to fasten the floatation processes. The application of coagulants increases the flocculent structure of the drifted particles, this processes helps to easily capture the air bubbles.

Floatation application can be broadly divided into *Dispersed Air Floatation and Dissolved Air Floatation.*

Dispersed Air Floatation – Air is introduced unwaveringly into the liquid by a revolving impeller or by applying diffusers. The air bubble thus formed in dispersed air floatation system are generally are found to be approximately in 1 millimeter in diameter and they generally cause turbulence which breaks up fragile particles. For this reason, among both floatation system, dispersed air floatation is not generally considered especially in the domestic waste water treatment. But it can be used for handling industrial waste water normally containing oil and grease.

Dissolved Air Floatation – Air is introduced into the waste water at a pressure of several atmosphere by which air easily get dissolved. Once it is achieved, the pressure on the waste water is reduced by using back pressure valve as a result of this it discharges micron sized bubbles. These minute air bubbles helps to transport suspended solid and oil to the surface of the floatation tank. The complete flow is pressurized and seized in the retention new bacterial cells. The introduced air is allowed to mix with waste water in the pressurization system which frequently degrades flocculent suspension succeeding chemical treatment. The time taken for completing this process in floatation tank is approximately half an hour.

b)   Secondary Treatment

The secondary treatment procedure refers to the natural biodegradation of organic matter by aerobic bacteria. In this treatment process, oxygen is delivered to the bacteria which is consumed under organized condition so that most of the biological oxygen demand (BOD) is removed in the treatment plant rather than in the whole treatment process. Thus, the principle requirement of secondary treatment process are –

- A sufficient amount of bacteria or microbes must be present in waste water to consume on the organic substances.
- Oxygen,
- Some techniques of achieving contact between the bacteria and the organic substances.

The widely used method for secondary treatment process are-

- Aerobic Treatment, and
- Anaerobic Treatment.

Aerobic Treatment-

This treatment involves two important techniques Activated Sludge Process and Biological Film System. Both will be discussed briefly in following sections.

Activated Sludge Process-

The activated sludge process was designed for the first time in England by Ardern and Lockett in 1914.

The essential features of the processes are

- Aeration Stage,
- Solid liquid separation following aeration,
- A sludge recycle system.

After primary treatment, waste water enters an aeration tank where the organic matter is brought into close contact with the sludge from the secondary clarifier. The sludge normally contains heavy amount of microorganism which are found to be in active stage of growth. Air is introduced into the tank in two ways – Either in the form of bubbles by using diffusers or by using surface aerator. The microorganism present in the sludge utilizes the oxygen and convert all most all the organic substance into stabilized and low energy compounds such as nitrate, carbon dioxide, sulphate. As an outcome the particles float to the surface from where they can be easily eliminated.

The main properties of Activated sludge are-

- It contains fertilizing constituents,
- Color indicates the degree of aeration,
- Under aerated sludge are light brown in color, and
- Well aerated sludge are golden brown in color.

The overall process of activated sludge includes five stages. The first stage involves the waste water aeration in the presence of microbial suspension. In the second stage, the separation of solid and liquid succeeding aeration. The third stage involves the discharge of clarified waste water. In the fourth stage, the excess biomass is reduced or wasting is conducted and in last stage the remaining biomass is return back to the aeration tank.

The prominent variables involves in Activated sludge process are –

- Mixing Regime,
- Loading Rate,
- Flow Scheme.

The end product of activated sludge process is carbon dioxide and it is basically a aerobic oxidation process.

Mixing Regime involves two important process – *Simple Plug flow and Complete Mixing*. This step is significant in activated sludge process as it influence –

- The requirement of oxygen in the aeration tank,
- The vulnerability of biomass to shock load,
- The local environmental circumstance in the aeration tank, and
- The kinetics prevailing the treatment procedure.

Loading Rate – There are mainly four types of loading parameters are available and applied which has been developed are as follows-

- Hydraulic Retention Time (HRT),
- Volumetric Organic Loading (VOL),
- Specific Substrate Utilization Rate (SSUR),
- Sludge Retention Rate (SRT), also known as Mean Cell Residence Time.

Flow Scheme – This involves three important patterns that is the pattern of aeration, the pattern of returning of sludge back to the aeration tank and the third one is the pattern of adding sewage time to time.

The conventional system usually maintains a plug flow regime. The important point is the loading or the amount of organic substance added comparative to microorganism available in activated sludge process. This ratio of food to microorganism is generally referred as Food to Microorganism Ratio (F/M). Inappropriately it is problematic to measure food to microorganism ratio, hence the ratio is usually expressed as the amount of BOD utilized per unit mass of dynamic biological solids. The combination of the liquid and the microorganism in the aeration tank is known as Mixed liquor and the suspended solids are called *Mixed liquor Suspended Solids (MLSS)*.

If the value of Effluent is small as compared to the value of Influent, Food to Microorganism Ratio may be expressed as,

Where, S_e = Effluent organic substance concentration,

S_i = Influent organic substance concentration,

Q = Waste activated sludge rate,

X = MLSS concentration in aeration tank,

Therefore,

$$\frac{F}{M} = \frac{Q\,(S_i - S_e)}{XV} = \frac{QS_i}{XV}$$

In another alteration of the basic scheme, aeration is strengthened at the inlet end and condensed gradually along the dimension of the aeration tank. This system is known as the *Tapered Aeration,* and it is the major enhancement in decreasing the cost of pumping air, as air is applied more successfully.

Biological Film Contractor

This involves two important process – *Trickling Filter and Rotating Biological Contractor or Rotating Bist Contractor (RBC).*

Trickling Filter –

A trickling filter is also known as *percolating filter or Sprinkling filter*. It is basically a manmade bed of stones over which waste water is permitted to sprinkler or trickle so that bacteria can able to breakdown organic waste. These are influenced by temperature, Cold weather lessens the biological activity in the filter.

Trickling filter has the decent adaptability to handle peak shock loads. The pharmaceutical industries, milk processing units, and the paper and pulp industries mostly uses trickling filter for the treatment of their effluents.

In this treatment process, the depth is kept at one to three meter with maximum openings or space lies between rocks to permit air to circulate effortlessly. The rock bed packing is coated with a biological mucus over which an influent is interspersed. As soon as the influent trickle over the rock bed packing, oxygen as well as the dissolved organic substance distributes into the film to be metabolized by the microbes in the mucus layer. The end product generated are carbon dioxide, nitrate, etc. which disperse back into the film and appears in the filter effluent. Gradually as soon as the microbes uses the organic matter, the thickness of the mucus film increases to a point where it can no longer be maintained on the compacted media and gets disconnected from the surface. This process is referred as *Sloughing*.

Trickling filter is widely applied for industrial waste as well as for domestic sewages. They are good in handling shock loads and its performance require minimum supervision. The tricking filter are broadly classified into two types on the basis of the hydraulic and organic loading-

- Standard Rate Trickling Filter *(Also known as Low Rate Trickling Filter)*, and
- High Rate Trickling Filter.

The *Hydraulic loading* is the entire volume of liquid applied per hour per unit surface area of filter bed while the *Organic loading* is the entire weight of five days at 20 °C BOD applied per day per unit volume of filter media. Organic loading is normally expressed as g/day/m^3 and Hydraulic loading is expressed as m^3/hour/hectare.

Standard Rate is also referred as Low Rate Trickling Filter. It has low hydraulic loading that is 525–2100 m^3/h/hectare and organic loading rate varies from 80 to 400 g/day/m^3 while these are significantly higher for high rate filter. These are suitable for treating weak waste water.

High Rate Trickling Filter have comparatively high hydraulic loading of 4200 to 15000 m^3/h/hectare and organic loading rates varies from 400–4800 g/day/m^3. These are applied for partial or roughly treatment of waste, before the waste is directed for further treatment. In this the application of waste water is uninterrupted, and the treated or partially treated waste water is recirculated. By this process, a portion of treated sewage or waste water is again returned back to the treatment process. In this way, high rate trickling filter operates generally in two or three stages with or without sedimentation between these stages. Comparatively high rate trickling filter is more efficient and reliable than standard or low rate trickling flow. Box 2.2 indicates the comparison of standard and high rate filter.

Box 2.2 Comparison of Standard and High Rate filter

Parameter	Standard Rate Filter	High Rate Filter
Hydraulic Loading (m^3/h/hc)	525 to 2100	4200 to 15000
Organic Loading (g/day/m^3)	80 to 400	400 to 4800

Advantages of Trickling Filter –

- The mechanism is very simple and it can be easily operates with no skilled supervision.
- This process diminishes BOD to the point of 70 percent, and colloidal matter to the point of 80 percent.
- The effluents so obtained are highly stabilized and nitrified and due to this reason it needed smaller volume of water for dilution.
- The electrical consumption is less for running mechanical equipment.

Disadvantages of Trickling Filter-

- Initial cost of construction of these filter is very expensive.
- The overall mechanism generates fly nuisance and offensive odor.
- The Trickling filter requires maximum land area for setup.

The comparative study between Trickling Filter and Activated Sludge Process is given in Table 2.2.

Table 2.2 Comparison between Trickling Filter and Activated Sludge Process

Trickling Filter	Activated Sludge Process
The bacterial growth is fixed on the media	The bacterial growth is suspended as a dispersed floc
All solids from the settler are wasted	The solids from the settler are partially recycled
Less sensitive to shock loading, it is more stable	More sensitive to shock loading, require closer process control
It generate insect and odor	It generates spray clouds
It is less effective in removing disease – causing organism	It is more effective in removing pathogens than trickling filter
Low operating cost	High operating cost

c) Tertiary Treatment

The prominent purpose of tertiary treatment is an effective and efficient elimination of pollutants than primary, secondary treatment and it can be applied at any stage of the total treatment, not inevitably after primary or secondary treatment. The main objective of tertiary treatment is to decrease the load of nitrogen and phosphorous compounds existing in the effluents by the following process-

- Precipitation,
- Nitrogen Stripping, and
- Chlorination.

Precipitation –

The discharge received after secondary treatment is mixed with calcium oxide or Lime. This lime then reacts with phosphorous compounds in the waste to form insoluble calcium phosphate which then settles down at the bottom of the settling tank from where it is filtered out. The pH required to complete this treatment process is in the range of 10.5 to 11.5

$$3HPO_4^{3-} + 5Ca2^+ + 4OH^- \longrightarrow Ca_5OH\,(PO_4) \downarrow + 3H_2O$$

In addition to this precipitation process, it further reacts with bicarbonate alkalinity of wastewater to form CaCO3.

$$CaH\,(CO_3)_2 + Ca\,(OH)_2 \longrightarrow 2\,CaCO_3 \downarrow + 2H_2O$$

Nitrogen Stripping –

In waste water nitrogen is generally exist in the form of nitrites, nitrates, and ammonia gas. Ammonia gas is highly objectionable in water reservoir as it is terrifically lethal to aquatic biota. Eventually nitrogen enhances eutrophication. The waste water with ammonia is directed into metal tower. From where waste water trickles downwards over a series of small plastic baffle plate and air is forced upwards through effluents which thereby result in the removal of ammonia gas. The two prominent methods of nitrogen elimination from waste water are-

- – Ammonia Stripping, and
- – Biological Nitrifying and Dentrification.

Ammonia Stripping-

In this process, first all the ammonia ion present in waste water is converted to ammonia gas. The reaction that govern this conversion are:

$$NH_4^+ + OH^- \rightleftharpoons NH_4OH \rightleftharpoons NH_3 \uparrow + H_2O$$

The free ammonia thus generated is then air stripped in a stripping tower. The ammonia stripping method is predominantly well suited to follow a lime coagulation process in which the pH of waste water is adjusted to approximately 9.5. However, further addition of lime is essential to elevate the pH to above 11. A major delinquent in this process is the formation of calcium carbonate scale. The scale formation can be controlled by regular maintenance, which consists of washing and scrapping the tower to eliminate scale. The ammonia elimination efficiencies at the pH value of 11.5 and 10.5 are approximately 86 percent and 80 percent respectively. However, elimination efficiencies drop significantly in cold weather.

Biological Nitrifying and Dentrification

In nitrification process, the waste water is thoroughly treated in the aeration chamber where all ammonia present in waste water is converted by bacteria to nitrate ions. This generally involves lengthier detention time and foods to microorganism ratio are maintained around 0.3. During nitrification process, bacteria such as nitrosomonas and nitrobacter, catabolizes ammonia to nitrate and nitrite according to the following two equation-

$$NH_4^+ \xrightarrow{\text{Nitrosomonas}} NO_2^-$$

$$NO_2^- \xrightarrow{\text{Nitrobacter}} NO_3^-$$

Both the microorganism needed inorganic carbon for synthesis and they are extremely sensitive to pH. The optimum pH required for nitrification is 8.4. The nitrite and nitrate forms are eliminated from the system by the process of *Dentrification*. It is an aerobic process in which heterotrophic bacteria found in activated sludge reduces nitrite and nitrate to nitrogen gas.

Chlorination –

The effluent or waste water from which nitrogen, phosphorous and dissolved organic matter is eliminated, is then subjected to chlorination to kill diseases causing microorganism that might be present in waste water. The main function or objective of chlorination is to:

- Assist the process of waste water treatment,
- Control foaming in sludge digestion tanks,
- Control pathogenic microorganism present in sewage treatment plant,
- Reduce BOD, and to eliminate oil and grease, etc.
- Prevent the spread of epidemics.

The quantity of chlorine applied varies from 20 mg/l to approximately 5 mg/l for totally treated sewage or waste water. Finally, the treated waste water is then discharged into water reservoir.

Other Methods-

There are several other methods which are available that have been used for advanced waste water treatment. These are Adsorption, Chemical Oxidation, Desalination, Chemical Coagulation and Micro-staining etc.

Adsorption-

This process are mainly used to eliminate offensive odors and unpleasant taste. Adsorption is considered as surface phenomenon and it was invented in 1881 by German physicist Heinrich Kayser (1853–1940). It is the process in which the adsorbate are transferred from bulk of solution to the surface of adsorbents. This process basically involves two process – Chemical adsorption or Chemisorption and Physical adsorption or Physiosorption.

In *Chemisorption*, the reaction is specific and energy requirement are also very high, ranging from 40 to 800 KJ/mol. The valence forces are involved in holding adsorbed molecules to the surface of the adsorbent in Chemisorption process. In *Physiosorption*, the reaction process are reversible, equilibrium is attained fast so the energy requirement are small usually between 5 to 40 KJ/mol. This involves weak vander-waal's forces to adsorb molecules to the surface of the adsorbent.

Box 2.3 Features of Treatment Process

Features of Treatment Process

a) *Primary Treatment-*
   The main aim of primary treatment process is to eliminate-
   * *Floating matter and Coarse suspended substance through screening,*
   * *Grit, that is, broken glass, sand etc. in grit chamber, and*
   * *Oily and greasy substances by floatation in skimming tanks.*

b) *Secondary Treatment-*
   The main objective of secondary or biological treatment process is to convert the remaining organic matter of the sewage into stabilized form by oxidation. The matter which settles down at the bottom after treatment is called sludge and the liquid is called effluent. In this treatment process, rest of the 45 to 50 percent organic substance is transformed into stabilized form by aerobic and anaerobic bacteria.

c) *Tertiary treatment-*
   The prominent purpose of tertiary treatment is an effective and efficient elimination of pollutants than primary, secondary treatment and it can be applied at any stage of the total treatment, not inevitably after primary or secondary treatment. The main objective of tertiary treatment is to decrease the load of nitrogen and phosphorous compounds existing in the effluents.

2.3 Industrial Waste Water Treatment

The industrial waste water treatment depends upon the nature and characteristics of waste. For instance, when the industry uses raw materials of complicated organic matter, generally an activated sludge process is applied for the treatment of such wastes. The Flocculation and Sedimentation is used for the treatment of tannery wastes. Trickling filters are applied to lessen biological oxygen demand (BOD) and to remove suspended solids, when brewery wastes are subject to be treated. Fermentation wastes are generally solid as animal food after proper treatment, which involves drying and evaporation method. The principle of industrial waste treatment is already discussed in previous chapter.

The common waste water treatment methods is applied for industrial waste such as, Primary treatment, Secondary treatment, and Tertiary treatment. These treatment methods are already discussed in previous section. The treatment process is selected for a particular effluent based on the quality of waste water. As the quality of waste water is uniform and predictable and the pollutant present is also known.

Besides acidic or basic waste are first neutralized and then proceed to further treatment process. For example, the acidic waste are generally neutralized by lime or calcium oxide (CaO). The lime is the most common neutralizing agent used in industrial treatment process. It is also cheaper and very effective. Basic waste or alkaline waste are neutralized with sulphuric acid (H_2SO_4). When the acidic or basic wastes are neutralized to a pH of 6.00 to 9.00, it can be directly discharged into the receiving streams.

Lagooning or storing of wastes reduces the problem to some extent. By storing or Lagooning it is possible to-

- Reduction in BOD,
- Removal of suspended matter,
- Self-neutralization,
- Equalization,
- Aerobic biological degradation,
- Anaerobic biological degradation,
- Settling, and
- Promotion of spontaneous and induced chemical reactions.

Tannery waste are dangerous to the workers of the plant also, as it contains high amount of causative agent of Anthrax. Paper and pulp industries waste are discussed briefly in next section.

Paper and Pulp Industries

The wastes they generate are mostly bit of bark, cellulose fiber, stray wood chips, dissolved lignin, and an extensive diversity of chemical compounds. During the manufacturing process, approximately 50 percent of the wood is disallowed as waste material directly or indirectly. These would later on produce sludge. Bleaching chemicals are also very toxic such as free chlorine, sulphur dioxide, methyl mercaptan, sodium pentachloro phenate etc.

The waste generated from paper and pulp industries are properly treated before discharging into water reservoir. In India, JK paper mills is considered to be the greatest paper mills because of the following features, they used in their industry-

- A modern pulping process,
- The quantity of bleaching chemicals and water is less,
- JK paper mill consumes approximately 12 kg of elemental chlorine per ton of paper produced in comparison to rest of the other mills, which consume approximately 100 kg.

A modern pulping process is also known as Rapid Displacement Heating (RDH). By this RDH, it is possible to lessen energy consumption and its fiber efficiency is also found to be of high quality. Besides the most important features of ecofriendly paper and pulp industry are-

- It must have a formal environmental policy statements and a committee to look after environmental affairs day today.
- Must have installed chemical recovery plants to recover chemicals in the waste they generate.
- Bleaching process must be in improvised state.
- Industry must have ETP in a proper functioning stage and also equipment to control emissions.
- Industry must have knowledge and capability of recycling and reusing of waste.
- Industry must maintain proper environmental auditing annually.

2.4 Purification of Water

The inevitability of water purification was known in India from very early time. The very common method applies in India is to keep drinking water in copper vessels or to boil water before using it. Most of the ill health is largely due to lack of safe drinking water. The positive community health and well-being is not possible without safe water supply. A safe water or the drinking water must be free from all sort of pathogenic microbes, toxic elements and it must be odor free and good to taste. The classical water borne diseases caused by the presence of a several aquatic host or infective agent in water. Table 2.3 depicts water borne diseases.

Table 2.3 Water Borne Diseases

Micro-organism	Water Borne Diseases
Infective Agents	
1. Bacterial	Cholera, Paratyphoid, E. Coli, Rota virus, Bacillary dysentery, Typhoid, Diarrhoea.
2. Viral	Viral hepatitis, Poliomyelitis
3. Helminthic	Roundworm, Hydatid disease, Threadworm, Whipworm
4. Protozoal	Giardiasis, Amoebiasis
5. Leptospiral	Weil's disease
Aquatic host	
1. Snail	Schistosomiasis
2. Cyclops	Guineaworm, Fish tapeworm

There are several ways to purify water such as,

a) Sedimentation,

b) Coagulation and Filtration,

c) Sterilization and Disinfection,

d) Softening of water,

e) Desalination, and

f) Removal of suspended solid.

a)   Sedimentation-

The modest method to purify muddy water is to permit the suspended material in it to settle through the process of sedimentation. The elimination of colloidal, dispersed, and coarse impurities from water is refer as clarification. These can be eliminated either using sedimentation or by filtration. The filtration involves the passing of impure water through a porous material which captures or retains impurities on its surface and allow to pass only pure water through it. The sedimentation process involves impure particle to settle by gravity on the bottom of the settling tank. Sedimentation process takes a lengthier time and it also requires settling tanks of large dimensions. Moreover this process does not take guarantee of complete removal of impurities.

b)   Coagulation and Flocculation

The coagulation process is applied to eliminate colloidal particles from water. The coagulation process involves the application of reagents to remove colloidal impurities. Colloidal particles are very fine particles of size less than 0.0001mm and it may be electrically charged. The water retains color is also due to the existence of colloidal substance. The turbidity also indicates the presence of colloidal particles. Thus, coagulation is mostly adopted when turbidity of water is more than 40 mg/liter. Through the process of coagulation, the turbidity can reduce up to 20 mg/liter.

The objective of coagulation is to create particles of larger sizes by accumulation of certain chemicals known as *Coagulants*. The most common coagulants applied are –

- Aluminum sulphate [$Al_2(SO_4)_3.18 H_2O$]
  It is also known as alum or filter alum. Alum contains approximately 17 percent of aluminum sulphate. It reacts when pH of water varies from 6.5 to 8.5. If water is not alkaline, lime or calcium oxide is added. The quantity of alum is decided on the basis of the turbidity and color of water.

Besides aluminum sulphate, ferrous sulphate ($FeSO_4.7H_2O$), ferric chlorides ($FeCl_3$) are also used as coagulants. The ferric sulphate works when pH varies from 4 to 7 and above 9.0 and ferric chloride works well when pH is either above 8.5 or vary from 3.5 to 6.5.

The process of coagulation depends upon several factors such as,

- pH of the medium,
- Water temperature, and
- Amount of coagulant used, etc.

The process of coagulation can be strengthened by the addition of special reagents known as flocculants. The basic principle involves behind flocculants is to neutralized the charge on the colloidal particles and fasten the process. Therefore flocculants may be regarded as coagulant of coagulants. The most widely used flocculants is polyacrylamide (PAA). Besides maleic anhydride, starch, activated silica, sodium polyalginate, copolymer of vinyl acetate are also used. The quantity of polyacrylamide (PAA) is decided on the basis of the quantity of the treated water, method of application, type and size of the water treatment plant.

c) Sterilization and Disinfection

There are several method available for sterilization and disinfection of water. Broadly it can be divided into two parts – Chemical method of sterilization and physical method of sterilization.

i. Chemical method of Sterilization

This method of sterilization and disinfection involves several techniques to sterilized water which are discussed briefly below are-

- Precipitation,
- Aeration,
- Ozonisation,
- Oligodynamics,
- Chlorination,
- Bleaching powder method,
- Chloramine process, and
- Iodine method.

Precipitation –

This is very modest method where impurities are precipitated using certain reagents such as lime, soda ash etc.

Aeration-

This is based on natural process in which the contaminated water is exposed to air, through bubbling compressed air into impure water eventually eliminating carbon dioxide, iron as iron hydroxide and bad odor. Aeration are normally considered are of two types – Natural and Artificial.

Natural aeration which occurs in natural water reservoir, when water either flows slowly in its bed or when it forms a water fall. This process causes oxidation which removes bad odor, and other impurities. Artificial aeration occurs by spraying water in the form of spray or fountain.

Ozonisation-

Ozonisation process enhances the organoleptic properties of water and does not involve additional process to eliminate excess bacterial agents. It also sterilize, decolorizes, bleaches and deodorizes impure water. Since it has no irritation of mucous membrane it can be safely used. An excess of ozone has no side effects. Ozone has a stronger bactericidal action than chlorine. It works better and faster on bacteria. These properties makes Ozonisation a better option than chlorination.

The treatment plant consist of a tower which is divided into various compartments by means of perforated celluloid partitions. The tower has two inlets at the bottom from where ozonized oxygen and impure water are allowed to enter through separate inlets while there is an outlet at the top from where the sterilized water is finally collected. The quantity of ozone needed to sterilized and disinfect the water depends on the degree of pollution. The widely accepted dose lies from 0.5 to 4.0 mg/liter. The ozonisation process is independent of the temperature of water.

Oligodynamics-

This method is also known as Silver ion method. Silver naturally has bactericidal action. For this reason, generally water are used to keep in silver vessels to improve the quality of water over a long period of time. There are various theories given to support the bactericidal action of silver. One such theory suggest that probably silver ion interferes with the metabolism of bacteria and thus kill them. However, this is confirmed that silver ion has a disinfecting properties which increases with the concentration of silver ion and with the temperature of water. The rate of chemical reaction increases with increasing concentration of the reactants and with increasing temperature. Silver water is prepared electrochemically has a stronger bacterial action than chlorine. These properties makes silver ion a better option to be used in oligodynamics method.

Chlorination-

It is the simplest and cheapest method of water sterilization and disinfection. It may be used directly or as a bleaching powder. An excess of chlorine is eliminated by *sulphites antichlor*. The process of chlorination involves the reaction of chlorine with water to form hypochlorous acid (HOCl) and nascent oxygen. Both hypochlorous acid and nascent oxygen are powerful germicides.

$$Cl_2 + H_2O \longrightarrow HOCl + HCl$$

$$HOCl \longrightarrow HCl + (O)$$

The hypochlorous acid reaches with bacterial enzyme to interfere with the metabolism inside the cell.

Bleaching powder method –

It is soluble in water to the extent of one part in twenty parts of water. Water is generally mixed with required amount of bleaching powder and this mixture is then permitted to stand for several hours for the completion of sterilization. It is inevitable to calculate the exact amount of bleaching powder required by the quantity of impure water in question, to avoid any sort of bad odor and disagreeable taste. The factors on the basis of which the quantity of bleaching powder depends are-

- Temperature of the reaction,
- Time allowed for sterilization,
- Turbidity of water, and
- Quantity of oxidizable material present in water.

A better bleaching powder generally contains 35–38 percent available chlorine. The quality of bleaching powder depends on the quantity of available chlorine. The reason is that on standing, bleaching powder undergoes slow oxidation and gets transferred into calcium chloride and calcium chlorate. Hence percentage of available chlorine in bleaching powder decreases on storage.

$$CaOCl_2 + H_2SO_4 \longrightarrow CaSO_4 + H_2O + Cl_2$$

Available Chlorine

$$6CaOCl_2 \longrightarrow 5CaCl_2 + Ca(ClO_3)_2$$

Therefore, it is necessary to determine available chlorine present in bleaching powder before its application.

Chloramine Process-

This process involves the addition of ammonia and chlorine to water, this result in the formation of mono and di-chloramines, which destroy all the bacteria.

$$2NH_3 + Cl_2 \longrightarrow NH_4Cl + NH_2Cl$$

$$3NH_3 + 2Cl_2 \longrightarrow 2NH_4Cl + NHCl_2$$

Ammonia applied is normally half the quantity of chlorine. Due to the long lasting effects of chloramine compounds, it is considered to be a better option than chlorine alone. But the process of chloramine is very slow in comparison to chlorine alone. The contact or residence time for chloramine in water must be of two hours.

Iodine method-

It is also known as iodinated method and mostly applied in swimming pools. A saturated iodine solution in water is applied for sterilization and disinfection. As the temperature increases, the concentration of the solution also increases. For instance,

At 1 ºC , the solubility of iodine is 100 mg/liter,

At 20 ºC, the solubility of iodine is 300 mg/liter,

At 50 ºC, the solubility of iodine is 750 mg/liter, and so on.

ii. Physical methods of sterilization and Disinfection

The physical methods which are widely applied are either boiling or exposure to sunlight and ultraviolet light.

Boiling-

Boiling is an age old practice. Normally 15 to 30 minutes boiling destroys all pathogenic microorganism. It is the most reliable and cheapest method of sterilization and disinfection which is widely applied for domestic purpose. However, the one disadvantage with boiling is that boiling also eliminate all the dissolved gases and provide it a flat taste. It can be applied for small quantity of water but it is not applicable for large quantity of water.

Exposure to sunlight and UV light-

This is the latest method for sterilization and disinfection of water. Sunlight is naturally helpful in destroying microbes. Mercury vapor lamps enclosed in a quartz container may be used as a source of UV rays for the sterilization of water. The bactericidal action of UV rays depends on several factors such as-

- Bactericidal energy, which is generally from 2000 to 2900 A° have strongest effect and regarded as bactericidal region.
- Quantity of microorganism,
- Amount of suspended matter,
- Optical density of the water or its absorbing power, and
- Morphological and physiological properties of microorganism

d) Softening of water

The elimination of hardness or the process of lessening the hardness of water is refers as water softening. The term 'water softening' is purposeful to the procedure whereby the hardness of water is eliminated, notwithstanding of whether it is temporary or permanent hardness. Hard water is one that contains a large quantities of dissolved salts of calcium and magnesium. Generally among the salts responsible for hardness of water, calcium salt is not harmful to humans but the presence of magnesium salts in large quantities damages the organoleptic properties of water. The maximum permissible limit recommended for magnesium oxide in water is 15 mg/liter. The hard water is not recommended for use in domestic as well as for industrial purposes mainly because of –

- In industries, the formation of calcium carbonate is economically problematic as it is not a good conductor of heat. It interferes in many process and fuel efficiency is drastically cut and boilers become completely out of services by local overheating due to boiler scale.
- A large quantity of soap is needed for washing. The calcium and magnesium ions react with soap as a result it generates insoluble precipitates, such as $(C_{17}H_{35}COO)_2Ca$, $(C_{15}H_{31}COO)_2Ca$ and similar salts of magnesium. Approximately extra 2.4 gram per liter of soap is required when the hardness of water is found to be 7.1 mg-equivalent/liter.

- The application of hard water damages fabric drastically and prematurely as it absorbs calcium and magnesium salts eventually making them brittle.
- Scale deposits on the surface of heat exchangers such as condenser, boilers also drastically reduces the efficiency of equipment. As a result boiler tubes in industries, begin to bulge and finally crack. Therefore, scale is required to be eliminated periodically.

  There are various types of boiler scale such as *Sulphate scale* which contains up to 95 percent of calcium sulphate and has relatively high heat conductivity; *Carbonate scale* which contains up approximately 90 to 95 percent of calcium carbonate and it has lower heat conductivity comparative to sulphate scale; *Silicate scale* which contains approximately 45 to 48 percent of silicon oxide and it also has low heat conductivity.

Broadly water hardness is classified into two categories-

  i.   Temporary or Carbonate hardness, and
  ii. Permanent or Non-carbonate hardness.

Temporary or Carbonate hardness and Permanent or Non-Carbonate hardness-

The temporary hardness of water is mainly due to the presence of dissolved bicarbonates of calcium (Ca) and magnesium (Mg) in water. This is also known as carbonate hardness and can be removed simply by boiling or adding lime water. This hardness is mainly due to $Ca(HCO_3)_2$ and $Mg(HCO_3)_2$ and it is responsible for alkalinity in water. Therefore, it is calculated by estimating alkalinity of a sample of hard water.

The permanent hardness of water is mainly due to the presence of sulphate and chlorides of calcium and magnesium and it cannot be removed simply by boiling or adding lime. Specific methods are required for removing permanent hardness of water such as Lime-soda process or base-exchange process. The permanent hardness is also referred as Non-Carbonate hardness.

The carbonate hardness (temporary hardness) and non-carbonate hardness (permanent hardness) together constitutes *Total hardness* of water.

Temporary hardness can be removed using any of the following method-

- By Boiling,
- By addition of lime water or Clark's process,

Boiling-

When the water containing temporary hardness is boiled, the following reactions occurs-

$$Mg(HCO_3)_2 \longrightarrow MgCO_3 \downarrow + CO_2 \uparrow + H_2O$$

$$Ca(HCO_3) \longrightarrow CaCO_3 \downarrow + CO_2 \uparrow + H_2O$$

The soluble bicarbonate of calcium and magnesium gets decompose on boiling and gets precipitated as insoluble carbonates in water and these can be eliminated from water by the process of sedimentation. But this method is practically not feasible for softening large quantity of water.

Addition of Lime water or Clark's process-

The Clark's process involves the addition of calculated amount of lime to the hard water as a result, the bicarbonates present in water gets converted into insoluble calcium and magnesium carbonate and can be removed from the water by the same sedimentation process. The following reaction occurs when lime is added to hard water.

$$Mg(HCO_3)_2 + Ca(OH)_2 \longrightarrow Ca(HCO_3)_2 \downarrow + Mg(OH)_2 \downarrow$$

$$Ca(HCO_3)_2 + Ca(OH)_2 \longrightarrow 2CaCO_3 \downarrow + 2H_2O$$

The carbonate hardness by this process decline to 0.7 to 1.0 mg-equivalent/liter.

The permanent hardness of water can be removed only by specific methods such as,

- Lime-Soda Process, and
- Permutt or Zeolite Process.

Lime-Soda process-

If the water contains sulphate and chloride of calcium and magnesium, simply addition of lime cannot removes the hardness. Soda-ash (Na_2CO_3) is required to be added along with lime to remove non-carbonate hardness and this process is known as *Lime-Soda process*. As a result of lime-soda ash addition in water, calcium ion present in water is removed as $CaCO_3$ and magnesium as $Mg (OH)_2$. This process can be applied for both temporary and permanent hardness of water and has been separated into-

- Cold soda-lime process, and
- Hot soda-lime process.

The Cold soda-lime process is applied for partial softening of water. It is not recommended for softening of boiler feed water as it does not gives zero hardness and the residual hardness also damages water tube boilers.

In the hot soda-lime process, the combination of raw water, seed-sewage and softening chemicals is heated near the boiling point of water. In this the reaction are faster and it quickly completes the precipitation process. As a result, dissolved gases are easily eliminated. The advantage of using hot soda lime process is that the process completes within shorter period.

When both the temporary and permanent hardness (total hardness) presents, generally sodium hydroxide is used and the following reaction occurs,

$$Ca(HCO_3)_2 + 2NaOH \longrightarrow CaCO_3 + Na_2CO_3 + 2H_2O$$

$$CaCl_2 + Na_2CO_3 \longrightarrow CaCO_3 + 2NaCl$$

But there is also a disadvantage of using lime-soda process such as,

- It can only be used for industrial purposes as in industries it is easy to calculate the amount of $Ca(OH)_2$ and Na_2CO_3 required to add in water and finally to filtrate it to remove precipitates, which is not possible in household.
- This process is also not applicable for all industries because it generally give water which is super saturated with calcium carbonate and it can be extremely serious in case of laundry.

Permutt or Zeolite Process-

Permutt is basically an artificial zeolite and it is also known as hydrate of sodium aluminum orthosilicate. Zeolite also refers as *Green sand* are used for eliminating hardness of water, and artificial zeolite, also known as *Permutt.*

Permutt ($Na_2O.Al_2O_3.nSiO_2.xH_2O$) is not suitable in water but it acts as a base exchanger when it is brought in contact with water having cations. Through this process Ca^{++} and Mg^{++} is allowed to percolate from water and thus it can remove both temporary as well as permanent hardness. Sodium present in the permutt is replaced by divalent Ca^{++} and Mg^{++} ions by following reactions-

$$Na_2Z + Ca(HCO_3)_2 \longrightarrow 2NaHCO_3 + CaZ$$

(Zeolite)

$$Na_2Z + Mg(HCO_3)_2 \longrightarrow 2NaHCO_3 + MgZ$$

$$Na_2Z + CaSO_4 \longrightarrow Na_2SO_4 + CaZ$$

$$Na_2Z + MgSO_4 \longrightarrow Na_2SO_4 + MgZ$$

$$Na_2Z + CaCl_2 \longrightarrow 2NaCl + CaZ$$

$$Na_2Z + MgCl_2 \longrightarrow 2NaCl + MgZ$$

The water which are softened using this process cannot be applied for boiler purpose but can be used for laundry purposes.

Methods for determining hardness-

Hardness of water is usually expressed in terms of the dissolved calcium and magnesium salts and estimated as $CaCO_3$ equivalent. Hardness can also be expressed as ppm (parts of calcium carbonate hardness in million parts of water). The value of ppm can be divided by 17.5 to obtain grains per gallon. Another way by which hardness can be expressed is Degree Clark. It is the number of grains of calcium carbonate equivalent present in a gallon of hard water.

The degree of hardness for soft water is usually 0 to 10 degree, whereas medium hard water has 10 to 20 degree, and hard water has 20 to 30 degree and extremely hard water has 30 degree.

The relationship between different hardness units is:

1° Clark = 14.3 ppm or 1 ppm = 0.07 °Clark

1 ppm = 1 mg/liter = 0.07 °Clark = 0.1 °French.

There are several methods available for determining hardness such as,

- Calculation method,
- Titration Method,
- Soap Method and
- Complexometric Method.

Calculation Method-

In this method, hardness is determined by calculation from the mineral analysis and expressed as calcium carbonate. The quantity of calcium present as carbonate is calculated and added to it the equivalent magnesium and any aluminum, manganese, iron, as calcium carbonate. The sum is expressed as the total hardness in ppm of $CaCO_3$.

Titration Method-

This is applicable for determining temporary hardness of water. It is calculated by determining the alkalinity of hard water as temporary hardness is due to the presence of $Ca(HCO_3)_2$ and $Mg(HCO_3)_2$. Both the quantity of $Ca(HCO_3)_2$ and $Mg(HCO_3)_2$ will give same alkalinity and total alkalinity will be same and expressed as $CaCO_3$ equivalent.

In this process, the alkalinity is estimated by titrating 500 ml of filtered water against N/10 HCl using methyl orange as an indicator. Being a very weak acid, methyl orange will ionize sufficiently only in dilute solution. Therefore, it is essential to add N/10 HCl to a large volume of distilled water containing the indicator, before end point is indicated. In laboratory, generally the quantity of acid is first estimated in a blank titration and finally the amount is subtracted to neutralize the similar volume of temporary hard water.

Soap Method-

Hard water will not provide lather with soap. When standard soap solution is added to hard water, a precipitation of calcium and magnesium will form. The process carry on as long as there is hardness in the water, and the end point of precipitation is indicated by sudden manifestation of lather. Both permanent and temporary hardness can be estimated by knowing the volume of hard water and standard soap solution having known quantity of $CaCO_3$ equivalent hardness.

Complexometric Method-

Both temporary and permanent hardness of water can be estimated using titration process with EDTA (disodium salts of ethylene di-amine tetra acetic acid), which react with calcium and magnesium ions and as a result forms a stable anionic complexes.

e) Desalting or Desalinization

This process is mostly applied to convert saline water (such as sea water) into drinking water. Desalting or desalinization involves complete or partial demineralization of saline or brackish water. There are various techniques available for desalinization such as,

- Distillation Method,
- Freezing Method,
- Forced Circulation Vapor Compression Method,
- Multistage Evaporation Method,
- Reverse Osmosis, and
- Electrodialysis.

Among all these, the promising technology for desalinization are electrodialysis and reverse osmosis. This chapter will briefly discuss these promising technology.

Electrodialysis-

In this process, the positive and negative ions are separated from a flowing current of brackish or saline water by allowing it to pass through ion-exchange membranes under the influence of an electric field.

The method is based on the principle that when direct current of electricity moves through a saline water in series of cation and anions exchanger membranes, by the rule, cations pass through the cation exchanger membranes and anion passes through the anion exchanger membrane. As a consequences of movement of cation and anion, the salinity reduces in one space and increases in the other space and so on throughout the stack. The water encompassing more salt is run to the side which is meant for collecting waste, while the water encompassing less salt may possibly either be recirculated through the stack or it might be passed through a series of stacks. By this process, saline water might be converted into drinking water. This method decreases the salinity of brackish water in order to make it suitable for drinking and for other general uses, but it is very expensive.

Reverse Osmosis-

The processes is based on the fact that water is squeezed out of the waste instead of taking the waste out of water. In normal osmosis process generally a solution is separated through a semipermeable membrane from a sample of pure water, as a result, water tends to move through the membrane to the solution side by the process refers as *Osmosis*. To reverse this process, osmosis is prohibited by using pressure on the solution side, that is, just equal to osmotic pressure of solution. The applied pressure, when surpasses the osmotic pressure, water moves out of the solution to the pure water side of the membrane. This makes the process reverse and refers as *Reverse Osmosis*. By applying the reverse osmosis process it is possible to convert saline water into drinking water.

In this process, saline water is filled into the top of the container, while bottom of the container comprises of semipermeable membrane, which is made up of polystyrene, ethyl cellulose, or polyvinyl chloride. By applying large pressure on the incoming saline water, the osmotic flow reversed and salt free water come out of it and releases from the bottom pipe. The major challenge with reverse osmosis is to find out strong semipermeable membrane to tolerate the high pressure required for completion of the process.

2.5 Pattern of Water Supply in Rural Areas

The safe and wholesome water defined by Fair and Geyer (1954) that it must be free from harmful elements, pathogenic agents and must have pleasant taste and odor free. The main objective of any water supply system are to-

- supply safe and wholesome water to the consumers,
- supply water in adequate quantity, and
- provide water readily available to the consumers.

Generally water supply design is based on proven data for daily water consumption. But in case of rural areas, there is no established pattern of practice which might be considered as important limiting factor.

In India, the main traditional source of rural drinking water are –

- Open well,
- Ponds,
- Private wells, and
- Small scale irrigation reservoirs.

Besides boreholes, spring are generally used as the source of water. The government of India actually addressed rural drinking water supply sector in 1972–1973 through Accelerated Rural Water Supply Programme (ARWSP). The second bigger programme started by government of India in 1986–1987, which was renamed as Rajiv Gandhi National Drinking Water mission in 1991–1992. This involves technology intervention and focused on water quality. The third bigger programme was started in 1999–2000 which includes community in planning, management, and implementation of drinking water related schemes, later scaled up as *Swajaldhara* in 2002. The forth bigger programme started by government of India emphasis on ensuring sustainability of drinking water sources involving Community organization and Panchayati Raj Institutions (PRI).

National Rural Drinking Water Programme emphasis more on water quality through Water Quality Monitoring and Surveillance. The National Rural Water Quality Monitoring and Surveillance Programme launched in February 2005, and now this programme has been merged with National Rural Drinking Water Programme (NRDWP). The salient points of this programme are as follows-

- Proper examination of all drinking water sources must be conducted twice a year for bacteriological contamination and once a year for chemical contamination.
- Under NRDWP, water testing laboratory is essential to be established. There is also given a provision of testing water quality at the primary health centers (PHC).
- Field test kits to be used for detecting any sort of chemical contamination at the site. Funds were provided for procurement of field test kits (FTK) under National Rural Water Quality Monitoring and Surveillance.
- The person who are trained under this programme that is *Anganwadi workers, ASHA, School teachers, social workers* will look after the surveillance programme to ensure water quality.

In India, in many parts of the states, gram panchayat and their sub-committee were taken full responsibility for planning, management, maintenance, operation, and implementation of rural water supply systems. The report of 2015 indicates that 88 percent of the total population in India had access to at least basic water. This comprises 96 percent in urban areas and 85 percent in rural areas. The term *'at least basic water'* is in used since 2016, and it is related to the previously used *'improved water source.'*

2.6 Pattern of Water Supply Projects

Water supply projects are the essential commitments towards providing safe and wholesome water to all. The projects are prepared after conducting extensive field survey work and collecting the proven data of the population for daily water consumption. Once the project is completed, it is sent to the competent authority for sanction of grants for implementing the projects. While planning water supply projects, it must be taken into consideration that projects prepared must be sustainable that is economical and efficient.

For successfully preparing water supply projects, following primary data's are required-

- Geological data,
- Hydrological data,
- Topography of the area,
- Legal data of land,
- Sanitary condition of the area, and
- Public opinion.

The factors on which the successful water supply projects are constructed are-

- Population,
- Per capita demand of water,
- Development works such as parks, public places, or institutions etc.,
- Industries,
- Existing water supply,
- Conveyance of water,
- Sources of water,
- Quality of water,
- Pumping units for treated works,
- Treatment works,
- Overhead reservoir,
- Distribution system, and
- Economy and Reliability.

The estimated cost of water supply projects depends on several factors such as,

- The type of sewer,
- The type of treatment required,
- The length of rising mains,
- The pumping machinery size,
- The design of reservoir, and
- The distribution system.

CHAPTER III

Sewage and Sewage Treatment Process

"Sanitary works starts at the point where water supply works ends"

– Anonymous

3.1 Introduction

Water supply system is always accompanied with a disposal of waste water. Rapid urbanization and industrialization has emphasis the necessity of sewer system, disposal and sewage treatment plants. A proper and effective sewage disposal system is essential for the well-being of any community. Box 3.1 depicts the flow charts of the process of sanitary works.

Box 3.1 Flow Chart of the Process of Sanitary Works.

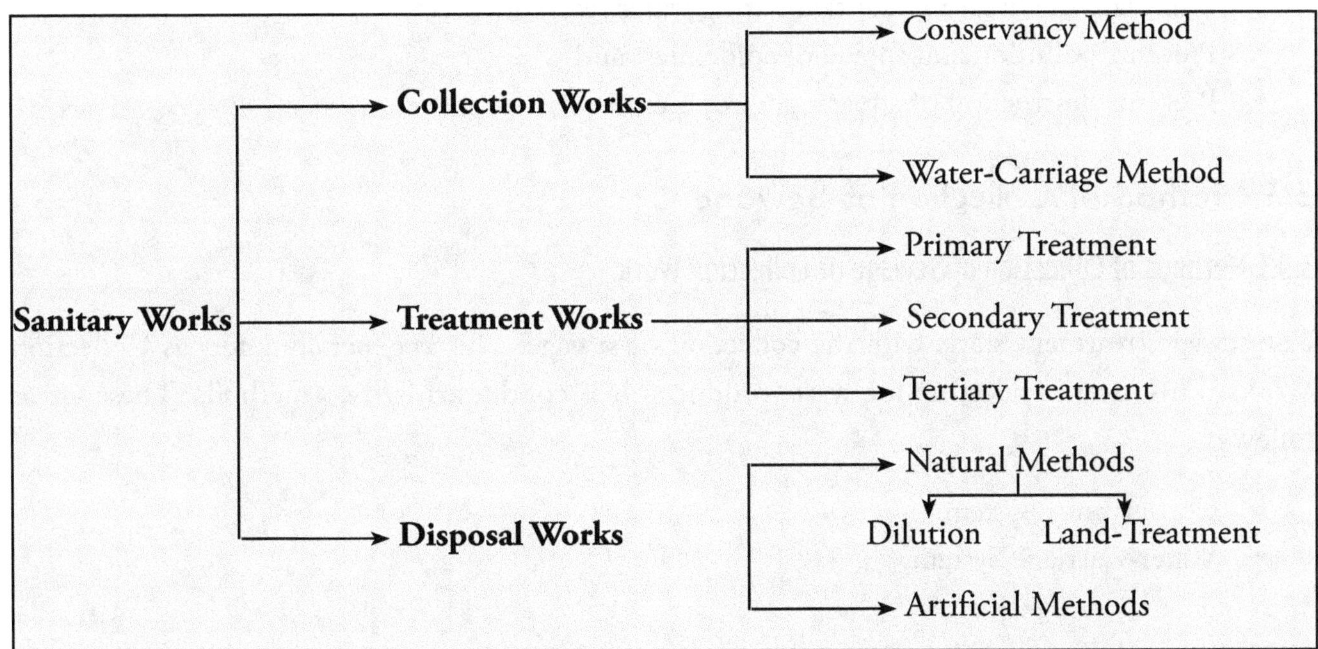

Raw sewage is generally composed of all sort of spent water or waste from kitchen, house, street washings, bathrooms, various industrial processes, dry refuse of house, and street sweepings,

75

semi-liquid waste of house and animal excreta, broken furniture, etc. Box 3.2 depicts the composition of sewage.

Box 3.2 Composition of Sewage

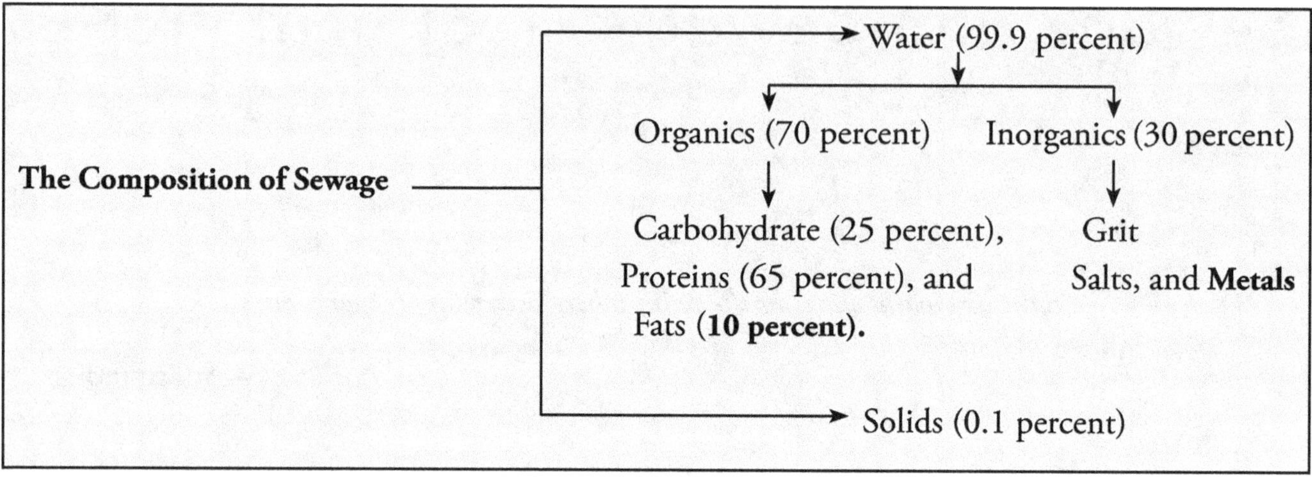

3.2 Resolution of Sewage Treatment Plant

The purpose or resolution of sewage treatment plant is the stabilization of organic matter. The *Stabilization Process* promotes the breakdown of organic matter or it stabilized the organic matter by converting it into simpler substance or inorganic form by aerobic decomposition.

The Sewage treatment plants assist to-

- Eliminate the hazard of contaminating water reservoir,
- Prevents pollution and spread of epidemics, and
- Prevents destruction of aquatic environment.

3.3 Method of Collection of Sewage

3.3.1 Methods of Collection of Sewage or Collection Work

The sewage treatment starts with the collection of sewage. This is generally refers as Collection Works. This means collecting the waste products. It is conducted by two methods. These are as follows;

- Conservancy System,
- Water-Carriage System.

a) *Conservancy System-*

This system is also known as 'Dry-System.' This is an age old practice where different types of wastes are separately collected and then each waste is disposed according to their characteristics. For instance,

– The night soil collected and then it is buried in trenches and covered with layers of dry soil and as a consequences, gradually it is converted into manure.
– The collected garbage is first separated into flammable and non-flammable matters. The flammable or combustible matter includes paper, dry leaves, etc. which can be burnt into incinerator, while non-flammable or non-combustible matter such as sand, dust, clay, etc. buried into low lying areas for the reclamation of the soil.
– The sullage or storm water are separately collected in open drains and finally disposed into water reservoirs without any treatment. It can also be used for farming or gardening.

The Conservancy method is not is used in modern cities due to various disadvantages such as,

– The night soil is collected only once in a day resulting in unhygienic condition as it undergoes decomposition process just after 4–5 hours of its production and major reason of spreading epidemics.
– The system is highly labour or human agency dependent and in their absence or any stoppage of work makes the locality or the area highly polluted.
– This process also requires large land area.
– The liquid waste could enter into groundwater and there exist a danger to pollute it also.
– This process result in insanitary condition which are hazardous to public health.
– The system is expensive in terms of maintenance and operation.

b) *Water Carriage System*

Rapid industrialization and urbanization promotes water-carriage system and this system replaces conservancy system. This system involves water, instead of human agency, as a medium to convey the sewage to the treatment area or disposal unit. This system does not use human agency to collect and conveyance the sewage. Therefore, the method in which water is applied or used for collection and conveyance of sewage is known as *Water-Carriage System.*

The sewage so formed contains 99.9 percent water and 0.1 percent solid matter. All these solids does not influence the specific gravity of the water as they remain suspended in the sewage. Therefore, it is easy to use all the hydraulic formulae for designing of sewerage system and the treatment plant. This system has several advantages in comparison to conservancy system in following ways-

– The procedure of this system is more hygienic in nature, as water is used as a medium for collection and conveyance of all the excremental matter. Therefore, there is no risk of spread of any epidemics.
– The land requirement for all the treatment and disposal of sewage is less in comparison to conservancy system. As one sewer in case of water-carriage system is placed which occupies less space in crowded lane.

- There is no nuisance in the street of the town due to offensive matters as all the sewage goes in closed sewers under the ground.
- This system is independent of manual labour or human agency.
- After treatment of sewage, it can be used for various other purposes such as gardening, farming, etc.

Table 3.1 depicts the comparison between conservancy and water-carriage system.

Conservancy System	Water-Carriage System
The set-up of system is economically cheap at initial stage.	The set-up of system is economically expensive at initial stage.
Since night soil are collected once in a day, therefore, it is needed to construct latrines away from the living room, so buildings cannot be designed as one compact unit.	There is no foul smell, latrines are clean and hence buildings are designed as one compact unit.
Large land area is required.	Less area is required.
The system is highly dependent on manual labour so there is danger of insanitary condition in the city in case of any stoppage of work.	No human agency is employed so there is no such danger or hazard of insanitary condition in the city.
Sewage is disposed of without any treatment so there is danger of water pollution.	Sewage is properly treated before disposing it into water reservoir.

3.3.2 Medium of Collection

It is also refers as Sewerage System which can be classified as,

- Combined System,
- Separate System, and
- Partially Separate System.

a) Combined System

It is refer to the sewerage system where only one set of sewer is placed for carrying both the sanitary sewage and the storm water. In this system,

- Flushing is not needed, As self-cleansing velocity is easily available at every place because of high quantity of sewage, and
- One set of pipes provides easy house plumbing.

But comparatively the initial cost is expensive and it is not suitable for areas where rainfall is heavy, and for a shorter period of time as the dry weather flow will be small due to which self-cleansing velocity will not be available eventually leading to silting up of the sewer.

b) Separate System

In this sewerage system, there is two set of sewer, one is for surface and storm water, and the other is for industrial and domestic sewage.

This system is economically cheaper than combined system because there lies a two separate sets of sewer for sewage and storm water respectively. The sewage flows in closed sewer and taken to treatment units while the surface and storm water flows in open drains and taken directly to water reservoirs. But in this system, self-cleansing velocity is not available unlike combined system, because of small quantity of sewage, and hence flushing is needed at several points. There is always remains a chance of mixing storm water with sanitary sewer and it might cause overflowing of sewer or gives heavy load on the treatment plant. In congested area, it is difficult to place two separate sewer.

c) Partially Separate System

This refers to the system where sometimes or deliberately a portion of storm water enters into the sewer carrying sanitary sewage, and the remaining storm water as usual flows in sewer carrying storm and surface water, it is called as Partially Separate System.

This system is considered as improvement over separate system. It is more economical, feasible and practical. It reduces the work of house plumbing as it allows storm and surface water to flow in the same pipe carrying sanitary sewage so no flushing is required in this process.

3.3.3 Pattern of Collection System

There are certain factors on which the pattern of collection system depends on-

- Proper information about the area is required for designing collection system.
- The hydrological and topographical features of the area.
- The type of sewerage system which will be used specifically in that area.
- The methods of treatment and disposal works.
- The exact location of treatment and disposal work.

There are several pattern suggested for the collection system such as,

- Perpendicular pattern,
- Interceptor pattern,
- Fan pattern,

- Zone pattern, and
- Radial pattern, etc.

3.4 Sewage Disposal

There are two important method of disposing off the sewage. Box 3.3 depicts sewage disposal. These can be classified as,

- Natural Process, and
- Artificial Process.

Box 3.3 Sewage Disposal

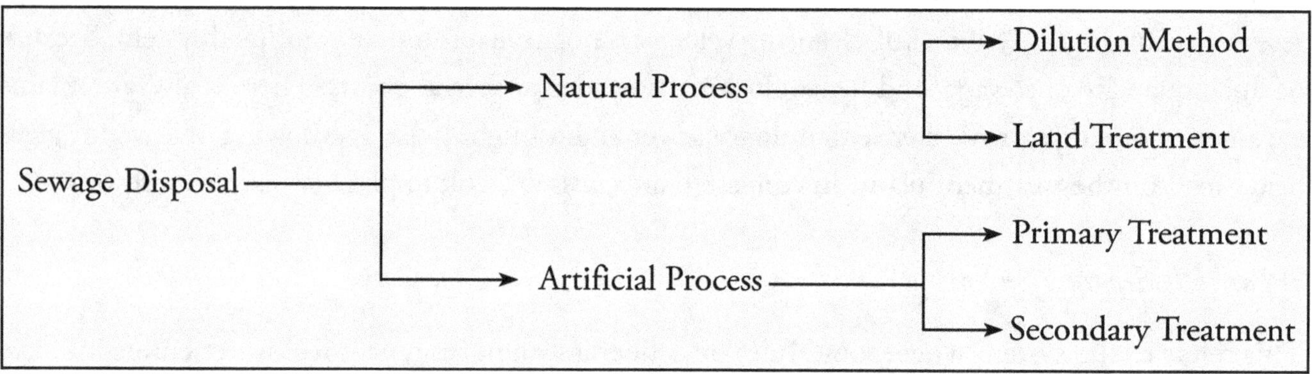

There are several methods of disposing sludge such as,

- Disposal on land,
- Drying on drying beds,
- Heat drying,
- Dumping into the sea,
- Distribution by pipelines,
- Incineration,
- Digestion followed by drying,
- Lagooning or Ponding,
- Press filters and Vacuum filters.

Sludge Seeding is the process of adding fresh sewage into the previously well digested sludge. Sludge seeding develops favorable condition for active bacteria and digestion occurs in a short period. The pH generally varies from 6.8 to 7.2. The digestion of sludge takes place in Sludge Digestion Tank.

Sludge Digestion Tank

In this, digestion is carried out by two types of bacteria. One group of bacteria attacks the organic matter constituting fats, carbohydrates, proteins, and convert them into simpler compounds releasing acids. These biological activity stops when acids accumulates in large quantity. The anaerobic bacteria starts their activity and convert the acids produced into methane (CH4) and makes the solution alkaline. It is, therefore, essential to maintain condition where both groups of bacteria survive successfully. The proper functioning of sludge disposal in sludge digestion tank depends on-

- pH,
- Food supply,
- Accessibility of the food, and
- Temperature.

This process is completed in three stages of acid production, acid regression, and alkaline fermentation stage. The sludge finally left is known as Ripened Sludge, which is alkaline in nature. This processes reduced BOD to satisfactory level.

3.4.1 Natural Process

These are mostly classified into two categories,

- Dilution, and
- Land Treatment Method.

a) *Dilution Method*

The disposal of sewage by releasing it into natural water reservoir such as river, stream, lake, sea, etc. Thus, the process of diluting sewage by letting it into a large volume of water is refer as Dilution Method. In due course of time, the sewage gets decomposed or purified by self-purification capacity of natural water. This method is successful only when-

- The volume of water is large enough to hold the sewage load safely, without causing any pollution,
- Water reservoir must be near the city or town.
- The quality of sewage must not be bad to make water unfit for any other purpose such as bathing, drinking, etc.
- The sewage quality must be fresh or non-septic.

Dilution method also gives primary treatment. The level of dissolved oxygen must be high enough to successfully handle the sewage load. The ratio of the quantity of diluting water to that of sewage is called *Dilution Factor*.

- If the dilution factor is above 500, sewage can be directly discharged into water,
- If it varies from 300–500, preliminary treatment of sewage is essential. The suspended solid should not 150 mg/litre.

- If it varies from 150–300, preliminary treatment of sewage followed by chemical precipitation is essential. The suspended solid must be less than 60 mg/litre.
- If it varies from 8–150, extensive treatment of sewage is essential. The suspended solid must be less than 30 mg/litre and BOD5 should not exceed 20 mg/litre.
- If it is less than 8, sewage required comprehensive treatment before discharging it into water reservoir.

b)   Land Treatment Method

When the sewage is uniformly spread on the surface of land, this process is known as land treatment. When sewage is spread evenly, part of sewage evaporates and the remaining portion percolates in the ground, as a result the organic suspended solids remain on the surface is acted upon by bacteria and partly oxidized in the presence of light, air and heat. The sewage has a fertilizer value, thus it improves the fertility of the soil of that particular area.

Land treatment is successful under certain circumstances such as,

- When there is no water reservoir nearby town or city to dispose of sewage.
- When rainfall is low and flow of water is also slow as in the case of summer season.
- When area of land used for disposing waste or sewage is mostly composed of loamy, sandy, or alluvial soil. As such soil can be easily aerated so aerobic condition easily prevails.

The term '*Sewage Farming*' is used for indicating the disposal of sewage by land treatment. The ability of soil to purify sewage depends mostly on physical, chemical, and biological actions.

- Filtration or percolation is the *physical action* that is involved in the purification of sewage by land treatment. The physical action depends on the nature of the soil. The porous, loamy, or sandy soil are suitable for land treatment method while rocky or clay soil are not suitable.
- When sewage spread on land, the *chemical process* of oxidation takes place in which organic matter of the sewage gets oxidized by soil bacteria.
- By *biological action or bacteriological action* the complex organic matter is gradually decomposed into simpler and stable compound forming humus.

Land treatment can be broadly classified into –

- Broad Irrigation Method, and
- Sewage Farming Method.

Broad Irrigation Method

An under drainage system consisting porous pipe of 150–200 mm in diameter are placed open. When sewage is applied or spread uniformly on land, it percolates into the ground, acts roughly as a filter. In the void of the soil, the organic matter becomes stabilized due to aerobic decomposition. The filtered water is collected in these drains and finally discharged into natural water reservoirs.

Sewage Farming Method

When sewage is spread uniformly on land, it is gradually converted into mineral salts by oxidation and biochemical action of bacteria. The waste water gets partly filtered through the soil. The mineral salts that produce have fertilizer value and so it increases the fertility of the soil.

3.4.2 Artificial Method

This method is broadly classified as Primary treatment and Secondary treatment. These methods have already been discussed in previous chapter.

3.5 Characteristics and Examination of Sewage

3.5.1 Characteristics of Sewage

Sewage is a dilute combination of varied types of wastes. The characteristics and composition of sewage is based on the sources from where it is generated like residential area, schools, hospitals, trade premises, laundries, or industries etc. Sewage contains mineral and organic matter as large and small particles floating in colloidal and in suspension form. Besides it also contains microorganism. The turbidity of water increases with the concentration of the sewage. The strength of sewer depends on the amount of waste and the per capita water consumption. As the daily contribution of solid matter per person per day will be different, might possible more or less constant, and the high dilution of sewage depends on the usage of water, for instances, high consumption of water will result in high dilution and weak sewage.

The characteristics of sewage is generally indicated by BOD, COD, total dissolved substance or total solids etc. On the basis of carbon to nitrogen ratio, domestic and industrial waste differ from each other. As in settled domestic sewer carbon to nitrogen ratio is much lesser than industrial wastes. Nitrogen is present either as ammonia form or in bounded form derived from proteinaceous substances. The ammonia contains approximately 50 to 70 percent of the total nitrogen. In domestic sewage, approximately 2.5 percent urea, 1 percent sodium chloride (NaCl) and other complex organic substance are present. It also contains nitrates and phosphates and phosphates of sodium and other builders, due to the presence of detergents or surface active reagents.

Besides the presence of microorganism (saprophytic and pathogenic microbes in high quantity) indicates high amount of biodegradable animal wastes, faeces, and household wastes in the form of organic compounds, such as, fats, proteins, carbohydrates etc. The characteristics of sewage can be broadly divided into –

a)   Physical Characteristics,
b)   Chemical Characteristics, and
c)   Biological Characteristics.

a)   The Physical Characteristics

This plays a vital role in identifying the characteristics of sewage. These are various physical characteristics, such as, odor, color, specific gravity, turbidity, temperature, and solids.

- *Specific Gravity* – The specific gravity of sewage is similar to that of the specific gravity of water.
- *Color* – The color of fresh domestic sewage grey or earthy. It has a soap solution present in it and once it starts decomposition, the color begins to get black and it happens minimum after 2 hours and maximum after 6 hours. At this point, it is refer as *stale sewage.* The color of industrial sewage be influenced by the chemical composition used and discharge of several industrial process.
- *Odor* – The fresh industrial sewage odor mostly influenced by the process applied in the industries while domestic sewage has oily or soapy smell and it starts giving offensive smell minimum after 2 hours of decomposition due to the release of hydrogen sulphides or other sulphur compounds.
- *Turbidity* – The turbidity of the sewage increase with the concentration of solid matters. This indicates the presence of solid matter in colloidal or in suspension form in sewage.
- *Temperature* – The temperature, is generally, slightly higher in sewage than in ordinary water. This happens mainly due to exothermic reaction which occurs as sewage flows in closed conduits, the viscosity and the bacterial activity increases, which eventually increases the temperature. Temperature influences the characteristics of sewage in many ways, such as,
  - The solubility of gases reduces as the temperature increases. A higher temperature impairs the process of self-purification capacity.
  - Higher temperature increases the biological activity, and as a result sewage gets stable more quickly and become septic.
- Solids – The composition of raw sewage indicates solids are present in 0.1 percent. In this organic and inorganic, both matters are present which contain –
  - Cellulose, fiber, cotton, starch as carbohydrates,
  - Fats and oils from kitchen, shops, laundries, and
  - Nitrogen compounds or protein wastes from animal, urea, hydrocarbons, etc.

Besides salts, grit etc. are also present. These are mostly present either in colloidal, suspension, or in dissolved form. Generally, suspended and dissolved solids creates more trouble in disposal of sewage while inorganic solids are not very harmful.

b)   *The Chemical Characteristics*

The sewage also constitutes gases, such as, hydrogen sulphides, ammonia, methane, carbon dioxide etc. generated either from decomposition of organic matter present in the sewage or from atmosphere. Fresh sewage is generally alkaline in nature, but as it under goes decomposition process, it becomes stale, acidic in nature. The industrial waste possess chemical properties and mostly toxic in nature.

c)   *The Biological Characteristics*

The sewage mostly contains microorganism due to the excremental matter present in sewage. Microbes also assist in sewage treatment and decomposition process as it helps to break complex organic substance into simple and stable substances. Based on the nature of microorganism, they are broadly classified as saprophytes and pathogenic microbes. Pathogenic microbes are responsible for spreading epidemics as they are very harmful and cause various diseases, such as, cholera, typhoid, amoeba dysentery, giardiasis, etc. The prominent source of pathogenic bacteria or microbes are night soil or faecal matter, urine and discharges from slaughter houses, industries, laundry, etc.

In sewage treatments, two types of bacteria are important, that is, aerobic and anaerobic bacteria. Aerobic bacteria convert organic matter present in sewage to carboneous, sulphurous, and nitrogenous compounds, when oxygen is either naturally present or artificially it is made available by the putrefaction process. The decomposition of matter using aerobic bacteria is refers as Aerobic decomposition, and the process is known as *Oxidation*. The treatment plants working on the principle of oxidation are-

- Aeration Tank,
- Trickling Filter,
- Oxidation Ponds,
- Intermittent Sand Filter, and
- Contact Beds.

Anaerobic bacteria starts their activity when aerobic bacteria die in absence of oxygen. Anaerobic bacteria also breaks down organic matter into simpler and stable substances without using oxygen or using little oxygen. The decomposition process which takes place in absence of oxygen refers as anaerobic decomposition, and the process is known as *Putrefaction*. The end products release in this process are ammonia, nitrogen, hydrogen sulphides, methane, amino acids, indole, etc. These gases are very offensive in odor. The indole produces extremely unpleasant odor. The treatment plants which works on the principle of putrefaction are,

- Septic Tanks,
- Sludge Digestion Tank, and
- Imhoff Tank.

3.5.2 Examination of Sewage or Analysis of Sewage

Before treatment of sewage, it is essential to examine the sewage due to the following reasons,

- To determine the strength, constituents, characteristics, and condition of sewage to be treated, and to identify the type of disposal work required.
- To improve the efficiency and performance of sewage treatment plants.
- To know whether the discharge received after final treatment is within the limit of self-purification or not.
- To know whether the effluents is safe enough to discharge into natural water reservoirs or need further treatment.

Sample Collection-

Sample collection of the sewage is the first step towards the examination of the sewage. For examination of sewage, the first step is to collect the sample of sewage. Since the composition of sewage changes with time and does not remain stable throughout the day, the samples are required to take at regular interval, at least at an interval of one hours over a period of twenty four hours. The volume of each sample may be range from 0.1 to 0.15 litre of sewage, bottle should be filled completely and air bubbles, scum, suspended matter, visible impurities, and sediments should be avoided. The samples should be protected from any outside contamination and should be properly closed and kept in a refrigerator. Preservatives, such as, sulphuric acid, chloroform are added to the sewage sample to protect it without changing its characteristics. Preservatives are added only if the examination are to be done for organic matter or grease. But for conducting BOD, no preservatives are to be added in the sewage sample.

The bottle used for collecting sewage sample must be properly sterilized before taking it in use. The analysis or examination of sewage should be started within 2 to 3 hours after the collection of the sample. Each sample should be properly labelled with details of –

- Source,
- Time,
- Date,
- Preservative added, and
- Collector identity.

Examination of Sewage

a)   The Physical Examination

This includes the examination of physical, characteristics, such as, color, odor, temperature, turbidity, total solids.

Temperature – The temperature is normally higher than that of natural water. If the temperature is below normal, it indicates the presence of ground or surface water. If the temperature is above normal, it indicates the presence of hot industrial wastes. It is generally measured by ordinary thermometers. The biological, chemical, and biochemical activities can also be determined by temperature as at warm temperature the biological activities are more pronounced while at low temperature these activities are mostly dormant. Thermometer should be capable to read up to 0.1 °C.

Turbidity – The sewage is turbid mainly due to the presence of suspended particles. It indicates the presence of solid matter as suspension, colloidal, and dissolved state. Turbidity can be determined by using Jackson's turbidimeter or turbidity rod, Hellige turbidimeter, Baylis turbidimeter, and HACH laboratory turbidimeter.

Color – Fresh sewage gives yellowish, grey or light brown color. Grey, earthy or soapy color indicates domestic sewage. Stale or septic sewage gives dark or black color. Color of sewage other than these color indicates that sewage contains industrial waste. The color of industrial waste depends on the process taken in Industries. To examine color, suspended matter presents in it are removed by centrifugal force in an apparatus and then the color is compared with standard color solution or color disc. The color generate by one milligram of platinum in a litre of distilled water has been fixed as the unit of color.

Odor – Fresh sewage normally has no odor but if it gives, it is mostly soapy or oily and not so objectionable. Stale or septic sewage has peculiar offensive odor, mostly of hydrogen sulphides, due to the decomposition of sewage. The offensive odor starts minimum after two hours and maximum after six hours. The industrial waste odor is influenced by the process taken in the industries.

By the odor or smell of sewage, it can be easily determined whether it is fresh, stale or septic. The concentrations of the odor are measured in terms of threshold odor number. The number is numerically equal to the amount of water in c.c.s required to be added to one litre of fresh odorless water.

b)   The Chemical Examination

The chemical examination involves the determination of BOD, COD, chloride and sulphides, chlorine demand, nitrogen, pH-value, grease, oil, total solid substances, etc. This chapter will briefly discuss the determination of BOD, COD, and Total Solids.

Biochemical Oxygen Demand (BOD)

BOD test was first proposed and designed by British Royal Commission of Sewage Disposal. It was noticed that all the river in England take five days to meet the sea and the mean temperature of river water in summer is usually 18.30 °C. Therefore, it was decided to have five days as incubation period, and 20 °C as an incubation temperature. Since these condition do not prevail or exist in India, hence BOD test in India does not give a clear idea of what is happening in discharge of wastes. Taking these points in consideration, in India and other tropical countries, the incubation temperature is shifted to 37 °C. However, still there are many limitation associated with BOD test.

The limitation of BOD are as follows,

- Preliminary treatment is essential if it contain toxic wastes,
- Applicable only for biodegradable waste or organic matter,
- High concentration of active bacteria is required to be present in the sewage.
- The effect of nitrifying organism are to be decrease before applying BOD test.
- Once the soluble organic matter is utilized or exhausted, there is no validity of the test.
- Time required for completing BOD test is long and arbitrary.

BOD is basically a standardized measurement of the amount of oxygen required by microorganism to cause the decomposition of organic matter in sample of water at 20 °C for five days. The result is generally refers as five days BOD, and it is expressed as milligram oxygen per litre of water (mg/litre) or in ppm.

BOD_5 value of raw sewage is 200–400 mg of oxygen per litre of water or 200–400 ppm. BOD_5 of drinking water is less than one ppm. BOD_5 value suggest how much oxygen is required to complete decomposition process. For instance, if BOD_5 is 200 mg/litre of water, this indicates that the biodegradation of organic matter in one litre of sample consumes 200 mg of oxygen.

$$CH_2O + O_2 \xrightarrow{\text{Microorganism}} CO_2 + H2O$$

BOD is an indicator and not a pollutant. It can measure any substance that can be consumed by microorganism using oxygen. Therefore, the substance that can be decomposed by microorganism can be either food or certain chemicals, such as, sulphate, sulphides, sulhites, ferrous ion, or any easily oxidizable compounds, which can be degraded using oxygen, perhaps with the help of enzymes produced by microorganism.

BOD examination can be influenced by –

- Type of microorganism (seed),
- Presence of toxic substances,

- pH value of water,
- Reduced mineral substances, and
- Nitrification process.

BOD_5 value is mostly required during measurement of treatment efficiency and operation, process design and loading calculation, pollution control, and determining the self-purification capacity of stream.

BOD Test

The sample of sewage water is diluted in water in 1:100 ratio, that is, one part of sewage and 99 part of water. The diluted sample is kept in incubator usually at 20 ºC for five days. The quantity of dissolved oxygen is measured in sample before and after incubation. The difference amount of oxygen before and after incubation, results the amount of oxygen consumed by the sewage. The BOD of domestic sewage generally obeys the law of the first order reaction,

$$v = kc$$

Where, v is the velocity of the reaction,

c is the concentration of the reactant,

k is the proportionality constant or velocity constant of a reaction.

The kinetic energy for the first order can be written as,

$$K = \frac{1}{T} \ln \frac{a_o}{a_o - x} \begin{pmatrix} a_{11} & a_{12} \\ a_{21} & a_{22} \end{pmatrix}$$

Where, K is the velocity constant of the chemical reaction,

a_o is the initial concentration of the substance (moles /litre),

x is the concentration of substance which has reacted in time T,

$(a_o - x)$ is the concentration of the remaining substance in time T (moles/litre), and

T is the time in days.

Therefore,

$$K = \frac{1}{T} \ln \frac{BOD_{2T}}{BOD_{2T} - BOD_T}$$

Then the total BOD is determined by the relation,

$$\text{Total BOD} = \frac{BOD_T}{1 - 10^{-KT}}$$

BOD rates can be calculated as follows,

The BOD rate at any moment is influenced by the temperature and the demand left behind to be satisfied.

If B is the BOD at any moment,

$$\frac{dB}{dt} = KB \text{ [Approximately at certain temperature]}$$

$$\text{or } \frac{dB}{B} = -k.dt \qquad \text{(Eq. 1)}$$

$$\text{Integrating log, } B = -kt + C$$

If the initial BOD be B_1 and after time t,

$$B_1 \text{ then, } \log_e. B_1 = kt + C$$

$$C = \log_e . B_{1t} + kt \qquad \text{(Eq. 1.1)}$$

Putting value of C in Eq 1, it will be

$$\text{Log}_e B = kt + \text{loge } B_{1t} + kt$$

$$\text{loge}\left(\frac{B_{1t}}{b}\right) = k(t-t_i)$$

$$B_{1t} = R. (e)^{k(t-t_i)}$$

$$B_{1t} = B. (10)^{k(t-t_i)} \qquad \text{(Eq. 1.2)}$$

Where, B_{1t} is the BOD at any time 't'

The demand exerted and the oxygen absorbed in time t will be,

$$= (B1 - B1t)$$

$$= B - B.10^{k(t-t_i)} = B = \left[1 - 10^{k(t-t_i)}\right] \qquad \text{(Eq. 1.3)}$$

Eq.1.3 formulae is applied when the water is heavily polluted.

The value of k in the Eq. 1.3 varies with the change in the temperature and is ascertain by the following formulae

$$k_T = k_{20} (1.047)^{(T-20)} \qquad \text{(Eq. 1.4)}$$

Where, k_T is the value of k at temperature T,

K_{20} is the value of k at 20 °C, and

T is the Temperature of the sewage in °C

The value of the initial BOD also changes with the change in the temperature and it is calculated by the following formulae,

$$(B_i) = (B_i)_{20} \, (0.02T + 0.6) \qquad\qquad (Eq. \ 1.5)$$

Where, B_i is the value of Bi at temperature T °C,

$(B_i)_{20}$ is the value of Bi at temperature 20 °C.

The value of BOD can be determined by Eq. 1.5 at any time and temperature.

Further, the velocity constant of BOD is influenced by the mass of microorganism, temperature, and ability to oxidize substance contained in a given medium.

Chemical Oxygen Demand (COD)

This determine the amount of carbon in organic matter of sewage. COD is more scientific in comparison to BOD. The time taken in COD test is far least than BOD test. This test is also easy and not influenced by any interferences, such as, fatty acid, nitrites, iron, chlorides, straight chain aliphatic compounds, etc. COD value is always higher than the total BOD. The reason is that not all pollutants are mineralized in biochemical process and the metabolites of cell microorganism, which are not mineralized by incubation have chances to return into the medium. COD is determined using stoichiometric equations, if only organic matter is present in sewage as well as amount and composition of pollutants are known.

The principle of COD is based on the fact that the organic matter gets oxidized completely by a strong chemical oxidizing agents potassium dichromate ($K_2Cr_2O_7$) remaining after the reaction is titrated with a standard ferrous ammonium sulphate of Mohr's salt [$Fe(NH_4)_2(SO_4)_2$]. The consumption of dichromate gives the oxygen required for oxidation of organic matter or the difference between the dichromate initially present, and the dichromate remaining unreacted thereafter provides the amount of dichromate used for the oxidation of organic matter.

Therefore, it can be said that the COD examination involves the oxidation of organic matter by strong oxidizing agent, and oxygen equivalent of the organic matter that can be oxidized is measured.

COD Test

A known quantity or measured amount of $K_2Cr_2O_7$ is added to the sample in the presence of sulphuric acid (H2SO4) and boiled for two hours. It is then cooled and the amount of $K_2Cr_2O_7$ remaining is measured using titration with standard solution of $Fe(NH_4)_2(SO_4)_2$. The dichromate consumed provides the oxygen required for the oxidation of organic matter.

The prominent features of COD test are-

- – It is determined generally using $K_2Cr_2O_7$ at a high temperature.
- – The oxidation of organic matter is enhanced or fasten by adding certain catalyst, such as, silver sulphate.
- – To avoid any interference in COD test, it is good to remove inorganic compounds in prior.
- – COD is always higher than BOD, as more compounds can be oxidized than can be biologically degraded. For instance, Fats and lignin are oxidized in COD test while due to its slow biodegradation, in BOD test these are not shown.
- – The limiting value of COD is 250 mg/litre.
- – Due to complex process and strong chemical used in manufacturing units, it has been noticed that it is possible to bring BOD within the permissible limit, but not possible to bring or decrease COD to the desired level.

Total Solids

Sewage contains organics matter which are mainly present in suspension, dissolved, or colloidal state. In sewage examination, it is essential to examine total solid present in it to determine the type of treatment it required. In the sample of sewage, most of the liquid evaporates leaving residue dried. The weight of dried mass represents the amounts of total solid present in the sewage. The solid can be volatile, non-volatile, or fixed.

Once the sewage sample is heated, the loss of weight due to heating represents the quantity of volatile matter and the rest represents non-volatile or fixed matter. The sample of sewage is passed through an asbestos filter. The quantity of solid in the effluents is calculated and difference in the amount of total solid present indicates the quantity of suspended solids. The remaining amount of total solid indicates the dissolved solids.

Therefore, Total Solids = Suspended Solid + Dissolved Solid

Total Solid Test

To calculate the amount of suspended solid in a sewage sample is made of Imhoff Cone. The Imhoff cone has a capacity of one litre and it is graduated up to 50 milliliter. It has a shape of conical glass vessel. In this Imhoff cone, the sewage is allowed to settle for 2 hours and then the amount of settled solids is noted. In order to ascertain the exact amount of settleable solids, the liquid is removed or decanted off and the collected solid at the bottom of the cone are weighed.

c) Biological Examination

The biological examination are conducted to know the types of bacteria present in sewage. This test is performed using microscope where the particular microbes are identified. Before identification, microbes are allowed to grow in favorable condition in culture media, which is kept in incubator at specified temperature and time. Once they form colonies, they can be easily identified using microscope. Bacteriological examination is essential to know not only the self-purification capacity of water but also the degree of pollution. The methodologies of bacteriological examination are already discussed in previous chapter.

3.6 Sewage Treatment Processes

The main objective of sewage treatment process is to decrease the sewage contents, and eliminate all the trouble causing elements in such a way that it can be safely discharges into the natural water reservoir.

3.6.1 Degree of Treatment

The degree of treatment is mainly decided by the regulatory agencies. The regulatory bodies set up the standard for the effluent and provide specific guidelines under which the effluents could be discharged into a water reservoir. These regulatory agencies can be local bodies and central or state pollution control boards. The method of treatment or sewage treatment procedure generally follows all these guidelines or standards and result in the maximum use of end products with economy.

3.6.2 Period of Design

Generally, the treatment plant is designed to meet the requirement over a period of 30 years after its completion. The time lag or gap between the design and the completion should not exceed 2 to 3 years, and in exceptional cases 5 years. It should be carefully examined whether liquid waste generated from industries does not adversely affect the treatment process so that it could be accepted, if essential with some primary or preliminary treatment and can be combined with the sewage from the community and can provide economical treatment.

3.6.3 Method of Sewage Treatment

The treatment process are broadly classified into-

- Primary Treatment or Mechanical Treatment,
- Secondary Treatment or Biological Treatment, and
- Tertiary Treatment or Advanced physical, chemical, or biological Treatment

These methods have already been discussed in previous chapter.

3.6.4 Layout of Sewage Treatment Plant

The following points should be keep in consideration while preparing layout of any sewage treatment plants. These are as follows,

- All treatment plant must be located in order of sequence. This would assist to transfer sewage from one process directly to next process.
- All treatment plant, if possible, must be located at such elevation that sewage can flow from one process to another process under its force of gravity.
- All treatment plant must be economical. It should not exceed the cost and must be cost-effective.
- Staff quarters and offices should be provided near the treatment plant, so that treatment plant must be properly and timely operated and maintained.
- It should be taken into consideration that overflow weirs and by-passes must be provided so that to cut the particular operations if desired.
- The self–cleansing velocity must develop at every stage. The site of treatment plant should be very neat and give good appearance.
- The over and all treatment plant should be economical, easy in maintenance, and should offer flexibility in operations.

3.6.5 Sludge Volume Index

The Sludge Volume Index (SVI) refers to the degree of concentration of sludge. It indicates the physical state of the sludge. It is basically a conventional measure of the settling ability of the sludge.

Sludge Volume Index is defined as the volume in milliliter occupied by one gram of sludge after it has settled in one litre cylinder for 30 minutes. SVI is expressed as milliliter per gram and it can be calculated as follows;

$$SVI = \frac{\text{Sludge volume after settling for 30 minutes x 1000}}{\text{MLSS Concentration}}$$

or

$$SVI = \frac{\text{Percentage of Sludge (by volume)}}{\text{Percentage of Suspended Solids (by wt.)}}$$

or

$$SVI = \frac{\text{Settled Volume of Sludge (\%) in half an hour}}{\text{MLSS (\%)}}$$

Sludge bulking can be avoided by-

- prolonged aeration,
- chlorination of sewage,

- increasing the pH of sewage to 8.0 or above,
- adding lime,
- reducing sewage flow to aeration tank for certain period of time, and
- reducing suspended solid concentration in the sewage.

The SVI of good sludge varies from 50 to 100 ml/g, but it may exceed to 200 ml/g for a poor sludge having a tendency towards bulking. The higher value of SVI indicates a fluffy and light sludge, and such a sludge takes a long time in settling, this indicates low efficiency of the process.

3.7 Miscellaneous Methods of Sewage Treatment Processes

Though the sewage treatment procedure is broadly classified into primary, secondary, and tertiary treatment, but on the basis of requirement, following miscellaneous treatment methods are applied with or without those treatments. These are,

3.7.1 Oxidation Pond

3.7.2 Aerated Lagoons

3.7.3 Oxidation Ditch

3.7.4 Anaerobic Lagoons

3.7.5 Septic Tanks

3.7.6 Imhoff Tanks

3.7.1 Oxidation Ponds

It is an artificial; pond of shallow depth in which sewage is retained and biologically treated is known as Oxidation Pond. It is also known as Oxidation Ditch or Lagoons or Sewage Stabilization Pond.

These ponds are applied for the treatment of raw sewage or partially treated sewage. In this process, under favorable climatic condition, that is, enough sunlight and warmth for the growth or proliferation of algae, the sewage is storage successfully. The aerobic acts on sewage and gradually convert or oxidize complex organic matter to simple, stable compounds and liberate carbon dioxide as end products. These liberated carbon dioxide is utilized by algae during photosynthesis process and liberate oxygen, which is used by the aerobic bacteria. The excess of oxygen in pond keep it in aerobic condition. Thus, in the oxidation pond, sewage is treated by the dual action of algae and bacterial action.

The retention or detention time of sewage in the pond is 2 to 40 days. On an average, 7 days is considered a better detention period. Oxidation pond is sufficient enough to remove BOD up to 90 percent and coliform group of bacteria up to 99 percent.

The design and selection of treatment by oxidation pond are influenced by following factors,

- Depth of tanks,
- Climatic condition,
- Incoming sewage,
- Temperature,
- Sunshine, and
- Rainfall.

The process is more successful and efficient when rainfall is low, temperature is high, and plenty of sunshine to fasten the process. The depth of pond should be between 0.9 to 1.2 m, it should be shallow so that sunlight can easily penetrate the sewage up to the bottom. The incoming sewage should be fresh and not be too strong. Due to overloading or unfavorable season, oxidation pond becomes septic and to avoid such condition sodium nitrate ($NaNO_3$) is added.

It is generally used in tropical countries where climatic condition are favorable for oxidation pond, and it is applied for small towns. This method needs no skilled supervision. The method is cost effective if enough land and suitable dry climate exists.

3.7.2 Aerated Lagoons

In a rectangular earthen basin, the sewage is filled into it. The natural oxygenation by wind is provided or supplemented with the help of mechanical aeration or diffused aeration. The raw sewage (that is the sewage without any primary treatment) is passed through grit chambers and aeration is supplemented with the help of high and low speed aerators or static tube aeration. The efficiency to reduce BOD is approximately 70 to 95 percent using aerated lagoons.

3.7.3 Oxidation Ditch

The procedure in the oxidation ditch is similar to activated sludge process. The sewage without any primary treatment is aerated by means of mechanical system and is allowed to settle down in settling tank. To settle the suspended solids, the aeration is stopped at least for two hours. This method has the efficiency to remove suspended solid up to 95 percent and BOD up to 98 percent. Finally the excess of sludge and effluents can be removed and disposed of without any further treatment.

3.7.4 Anaerobic Lagoons

Anaerobic ponds or lagoons are deep, up to the depth of more than 2 m. In this method, the suspended settle down at the bottom which is then subject to anaerobic decomposition. Besides algae and bacteria which are present at the surface, interact in aerobic conditions. And a layer of facultative bacteria present above the sludge, has the ability to oxidize the incoming organic matter and the products of digestion of the lower layer. These anaerobic lagoons are usually used for the treatment of warm and strong industrial wastes, but in this the effluent requires further treatment before discharging it into the natural water reservoir.

3.7.5 Septic Tank

Septic Tanks are used for disposing sewage received from small institutions, hotels, or some isolated buildings, etc. Septic tank refers to a water tight single storey tank where sewage is retained or detained for sufficiently long time to allow sedimentation. It works like a plain sedimentation tank. In this the settled sludge and the supernatant liquid go through anaerobic digestion. The Septic tank is completely closed tank, as it is covered at the top to avoid offensive odor released during the digestion or decomposition period of sludge. The Septic tank should be carefully constructed to enhance its performance.

The septic tank has the ability to eliminate up to 90 percent of BOD and 80 percent of suspended solid. Septic tank is not applicable for treating sewage on a large scale. The effluents discharged from the septic tank required further treatment before discharging it into the natural water reservoir. There are several methods to dispose effluents discharged from septic tanks, such as,

- Soak Pits,
- Adsorption trenches,
- Gardening,
- Soak wells,
- Natural water reservoirs,
- Subsoil irrigation,
- Trickling Filter,
- Surface Irrigation, etc.

3.7.6 Imhoff Tank

Imhoff Tank is also known as Two-storey digestion tank. It was proposed by German Scientist Karl Imhoff in 1906. Basically it is an improvement on the plain septic tank.

It is type of sludge digestion tank where both sedimentation and sludge digestion takes place in the same structure. The Imhoff tank consist of two separate compartments. In one compartment sediments takes place while in other sludge digestion. The incoming sewage lies in upper compartment where sedimentation takes place and this chamber is known as *Sedimentation Chamber*. In the lower chamber, the solids obtained from the sedimentation chamber are digested and this chamber is refer as *Digestion Chamber*.

These two chambers or compartments are separated by partition with sloping openings at 60 degree to the horizontal or slots at the bottom by which solids that are settled in the upper chamber, easily slide down to the lower chamber or compartments. The portion lies between upper and lower chamber is regarded as *Neutral Zone.*

The digested sludge from the bottom chamber is released or removed under hydrostatic pressure by a sludge outlet pipe. *Gas Vent or Scum Chamber* is the portion given above the neutral zone and by the side of sedimentation compartment to collect the gases formed in the digestion compartment and from here the gases are either escape into the atmosphere or can be used for some useful purpose. The principle gas released is methane (CH_4). The process of sludge digestion in Imhoff tank is better than Septic tank. Imhoff tank are suitable for small cities, institutions, etc.

CHAPTER IV

Self-Purification of Natural Water

'Water is worth for the life on the earth'

– Anonymous

Naturally water has self-purification capacity. There lies a balance between aquatic animals and plant life. When sewage is released into water reservoir, naturally the organic substances present in the sewage is oxidized by the microbes using dissolved oxygen content of water. This oxidation process is habitually carried out by microbes in which they break down the complex organic matter into simpler substances such as carbohydrates, sulphate, nitrates, ammonia etc. These substances are taken by microscopic zooplankton such as protozoa, which are in turn eaten by insects, fish etc. During this whole process, whatever the oxygen depletion occurs is counter balance by the absorption of oxygen from the atmosphere. In natural environment, therefore lies a perfect balance where utilization of oxygen by microbes for degrading sewage is automatically refilled by the atmosphere. This complete process is known as *Self-Purification of Natural water.*

The requirement of oxygen for self-purification is obtained from the atmosphere. For instance, Rain water gets mixed with natural water. Rain water which is saturated with atmospheric oxygen and thus on coming in contact with water reservoir, it increases the dissolved oxygen content of natural water. Besides the surface of water absorbs oxygen directly from the atmosphere and through diffusion or circulation of water, it is transferred to deeper water. Normally lower the temperature, the greater is the oxygen retaining capacity of water, whether it is fresh water or marine water.

The deepest layer of water generally have low oxygen concentration comparative to upper layer. This is mainly because of respiration of aquatic organism, decomposition of organic material or debris and complete absence of photosynthetic activity.

The self-purification become apparent in all natural water. The rate of self-purification depends on several factors such as —

- Rate of re-aeration,
- Temperature,
- Rate of Flow,
- Salinity,
- Type of organic matter introduced,
- Presence of dissolved oxygen in natural water,
- Sedimentation, etc.

Naturally, water currents also plays a vital role as they disperse the sewage as soon as it enters into water bodies. Besides the sunlight also acts as disinfectant and encourages the growth of algae by the process of photosynthesis. Algae releases oxygen during daylight and consumes oxygen during night. Hence water having algal growth is well saturated with oxygen during daylight and is also generous for the growth of bacteria.

Comparatively it is reported that shallow ponds have better self-purification devices. But as it is a known fact that both the solubility of oxygen and the rate of bacterial action depends on temperature. Therefore, dissolved oxygen is less in summer and during this warm season bacteria needed more oxygen, which increases oxygen demand. Due to this re-aeration become very slow, and thus temperature is considered to be a very important factor that influence the self-purification capacity of water.

When the discharge of organic matter increases rapidly due to human activities, the oxygen depletion increases eventually leading to high demand of oxygen by aquatic plants and animals. The absence of oxygen influences the degradation process of organic matter present in sewage, and thus the sewage content gradually started increasing in water bodies beyond their capacity. This whole process abruptly influence the self-purification capacity of water. It may cause pollution of water reservoir.

The process of self-purification are all physical, chemical, and biological in nature which involves-

- Dilution,
- Reduction,
- Oxidation,
- Sedimentation, and
- Sunlight.

Among all these, for self-purification dilution is very important method which greatly reduces the annoyance caused by obnoxious organic matter present in the sewage. The organic matter is readily oxidized by bacteria using dissolved oxygen. As per principle, the water reservoir which has the capacity to absorb oxygen as fast as possible, can purify itself in shorter time even if heavily polluted sewage is discharge into water stream. Aerobic condition is needed to be maintain for preventing any serious pollution of the stream.

CHAPTER V

Effluent Treatment Plant (ETP) and Sewage Treatment Plant (STP)

"Wastewater treatment is an Art, not Science"

– Prof. W.W. Eckenfelder

5.1 General Introduction

Industries uses water for various processes and after processing as a byproduct, it also generate wastewater, known as effluent which usually contains several pollutants. The treatment of these effluents are conducted in Effluent Treatment Plant, refer as ETP. On a daily basis, a huge quantity of sewage is generated from municipalities which need to be treated before discharging into water reservoir to avert cycling of pollution in an environment. This treatment is done in Sewage Treatment Plant, usually refer as STP.

The designing of ETP or STP required proper planning which starts right from water supply system and end by discharging safe treated water back to water reservoir or the user, based on demand. The planning can be done at national level, state level, and region or community level, based on the requirement. Waste water which is needed to be treated may differ both in quality and quantity, therefore, the degree of treatment required sometimes hourly, seasonally, daily, monthly, and yearly, also vary accordingly. The quality standards are set up by Ministry of Environment and Forest (MEF), Government of India, as per Environment Protection Rules, 1986, for inlet effluent, treated effluent, and general water quality standards as per IS 10500–1991, which are depicted in Table 5.1, 5.2, and 5.3.

101

Table 5.1 Quality Standards for Inlet Effluent of Common Effluent Treatment Plant.

Parameters	Standards (Concentration in mg/L)
pH	5.5–9.0
Temperature	45 °C
Oil and Grease	20
Phenolic Compounds	5
Ammonical Nitrogen	50
Heavy Metals	
Arsenic (As)	0.2
Mercury (Hg)	0.01
Cadmium (Cd)	1
Selenium (Se)	0.05
Fluoride (F)	15
Boron (B)	2
Chromium (Cr)	2
Copper (Cu)	3
Lead (Pb)	1
Nickel (Ni)	3
Zinc (Zn)	15
Radioactive Materials	
Alpha emitter	10–7 Hc/mL
Beta emitter	10–8 He/mL

(Source: Ministry of Environment and Forest, Government of India)

This is applicable mostly for small scale industries which daily discharges up to 25 KL/day.

Table 5.2 Quality Standard for Treated Effluent of Common Effluent Treatment Plant

Parameters	Into Inland Surface Water (Concentration in mg/L)	On land for Irrigation (Concentration in mg/L)	Into Marine Coastal areas (Concentration in mg/L)
pH	5.5–9.0	5.5–9.0	5.5–9.0
Temperature	Should not be more than 40 °C in any section of the stream within 15mt down steam from the outlet.	–	45 °C at the point of discharge
BOD (Three days at 27 °C)	30	100	100
COD	250	–	250

Parameters	Into Inland Surface Water (Concentration in mg/L)	On land for Irrigation (Concentration in mg/L)	Into Marine Coastal areas (Concentration in mg/L)
Oil and Grease	10	10	20
Suspended Solid	100	200	For process waste water it is 100
Dissolved Substance (Inorganic)	2100	2100	–
Total Residue Chlorine	1	–	1
Ammonical Nitrogen	50	–	50
Total Kjeldahl Nitrogen	100	–	100
Pesticides	Absent	Absent	Absent
Heavy Metals			
Arsenic	0.2	0.2	0.2
Sulphate (SO4)	2.8	–	5.0
Fluoride (F)	2.0	–	15
Mercury (Hg)	0.01	–	0.01
Lead (Pb)	0.1	–	1.0
Cadmium (Cd)	1.0	–	2.0
Chromium (Cr)	2.0	–	2.0
Copper (Cu)	3.0	–	3.0
Zinc (Zn)	5	–	15
Selenium (Se)	0.05	–	0.05
Boron (B)	2.0	2.0	–
Cyanide (CN)	0.2	0.2	0.2
Chlorine (Cl)	1000	600	–
Percent Sodium	–	60	–

(Source: Ministry of Environment and Forest, Government of India)

Table 5.3 Water Quality Standard (as per IS 10500–1991)

Parameters	Desirable (mg/L)	Permissible (mg/L)	Risk/ Human Health Hazards	Source	Treatment Required
pH	6.5–8.5	No Relaxation	Low pH (Acidic) – Metallic taste or Corrosion High pH (Alkaline) – Soda or Bitter taste, deposits.	Natural sources, sometimes artificial sources	Increase pH (Alkaline) by Soda ash and Decrease pH (Acidic) by vinegar or citric acid.
Color	5 Hazen Unit (Hz)	25 Hz	Visible tint	Iron, Copper, Manganese, Tannins, Natural deposits.	Distillation, Filtration, Ozonisation, and Reverse Osmosis.
Odor	Un objectionable	Unobjectionable	Rotten egg, Chemical or Musty	Hydrogen sulfide, Organic matter, Chlorine, Septic contamination and Methane gas	Activated carbon, Oxidation, Filtration, and Air Stripping.
Total Dissolved Substance (TDS)	500	2000	Hardness, Scaly deposits, Sediment, Staining, Salty and bitter taste, Corrosion of pipes and fittings, and Cloudy Colored water	Septic system, Livestock waste, Landfills, Hazardous waste landfills, Dissolved minerals, Iron and manganese, and nature of soil.	Distillation, Reverse Osmosis, and Deionization by Ion Exchange.

Parameters	Desirable (mg/L)	Permissible (mg/L)	Risk/ Human Health Hazards	Source	Treatment Required
Hardness	300	600	Scale in utensils and hot water system, soap scums.	Dissolved calcium and magnesium from soil and aquifer minerals containing dolomite or limestone	Water softener ion exchanger, and Reverse osmosis.
Alkalinity	200	600	Low alkalinity (Acidic condition) results in deterioration of plumbing and increases the chances of heavy metals.	Pipes, Hazardous waste landfills, and Landfills	Neutralizing agents
Heavy Metals					
Iron (Fe)	0.3	1.0	Brackish color, bitter or metallic taste, rusty sediments, iron bacteria, brown green stains.	Leaching of cast iron pipes in water distribution system.	Oxidizing filter, and Greensand mechanical filter.
Manganese (Mn)	0.1	0.3	Brownish color, black stains on laundry, bitter taste, altered taste of water mixed beverages.	Landfills deposits in soil.	Ion exchange, chlorination, green sand mechanical filter, and oxidizing filter.

(Cont.)

Parameters	Desirable (mg/L)	Permissible (mg/L)	Risk/ Human Health Hazards	Source	Treatment Required
Sulphate (SO_4)	200	400	Bitter or medicinal taste, scaly deposits, corrosion.	Animal sewage, septic system, by product of coal mining, industrial waste.	Ion exchange, Reverse osmosis, and Distillation
Nitrate (NO_3)	45	100	Methaemoglobinaemia or blue baby disease in infants	Livestock facilities, manure lagoons, septic system, Household waste water, fertilizer.	Iron Exchange, Reverse Osmosis, Distillation.
Chloride (Cl)	250	1000	Salty taste, blackening and pitting of stainless steel, corroded pipes, and High blood pressure.	Fertilizers, Industrial wastes, minerals.	Reverse osmosis, Activated carbon, and distillation
Fluoride (F)	1.0	1.5	Brownish discoloration of teeth, and bone damage	Industrial waste and geogenic sources	Activated alumina, Ion exchange, Reverse osmosis, and Distillation.

Parameters	Desirable (mg/L)	Permissible (mg/L)	Risk/ Human Health Hazards	Source	Treatment Required
Arsenic (As)	0.01	No Relaxation but as per Bureau of Indian Standards (BIS) it can be relax up to 0.05	Weight loss, nausea, gastrointestinal troubles, keratosis, melanosis, and skin cancer in chronic cases.	Natural sources such as fossil fuels, weathering of sedimentary rocks, and artificial sources such as metal refining process, by product of mining, burning of fossil fuel.	Reverse Osmosis, Activated alumina filtration, distillation, Chemical precipitation, lime softening, and ion exchange.
Chromium (Cr)	0.05	No Relaxation	Skin irritation, lung tumors, nasal ulcers, damage to the nervous system and circulatory system, accumulates in spleen, bones, kidney and liver.	Industrial discharges or waste, and mining sites	Reverse osmosis, distillation, and ion exchange
Copper (Cu)	0.05	1.5	Anemia, liver and kidney damage, gastrointestinal irritations, bitter or metallic taste, and blue green stains.	Leaching from copper water pipes and tubing, industrial and mining waste, wood preservatives and algae treatment.	Ion Exchange, Distillation and Reverse osmosis.

(Cont.)

Parameters	Desirable (mg/L)	Permissible (mg/L)	Risk/ Human Health Hazards	Source	Treatment Required
Cyanide (CN)	0.05	No Relaxation	Thyroid, and nervous system damages.	Fertilizer, electronics, steel, plastic mining.	Reverse osmosis, Chlorination, and Ion exchange.
Lead (Pb)	0.05	No Relaxation	Reduces mental capacity or mental retardation, hearing loss, hypertension, blood disorders.	Paints, Diesel fuel combustion, pipes and solder, leaded gasoline, discarded batteries.	Activated carbon, Ion exchange, Reverse osmosis, Distillation.
Mercury (Hg)	0.001	No Relaxation	Loss of vision and hearing, kidney and nervous system disorders, intellectual deterioration.	Fungicides, Batteries, Electrical equipment, Mining, Paper and pulp industries.	Reverse osmosis, and Distillation
Zinc (Zn)	5	15	Metallic taste.	Leaching of galvanized pipes and fittings, paints, and dyes.	Ion Exchangers, water softeners, Reverse osmosis, and distillation.
Total Coliform Bacteria	95 percent of samples should not contain coliform in 100 mL	No relaxation	Gastrointestinal diseases	Livestock facilities, manure lagoons, septic system, household waste water.	Chlorination, Distillation, and Iodination.

| E. Coliform Bacteria | Nil per 100 mL | No Relaxation | Gastrointestinal diseases | Livestock facilities, septic system, manure lagoons, household waste water | Distillation, Iodination, and Chlorination |

(Source: Ministry of Environment and Forest, Government of India)

Any planning of ETP or STP is based on the area and population to be served, the design period, the per capita rate of water supply, the utilization of centralized and multiple points of treatment facilities. Plants are required to be properly identified and prepared in adequate detail in order to implement it timely and properly. Optimization of planning is required to be done by taking number of factors into consideration, such as, the degree of treatment to be provided by determining the capacities of several units, capital cost required, interest charges, water tax, and water rate. The planning of treatment plant is based on three important fundamental principles –

- Proper Design,
- Proper Engineering, and
- Proper Operation and Maintenance.

The design is a primary stage in any wastewater treatment process in which the foremost step is to analyze the untreated waste water and based on the requirement of uses of treated effluent, treatment plant is designed. After this stage, engineering decisions are required to specify the area, industry, and population to be served. Besides the design period, the per capita rate of water supply, the nature of wastewater, location of facilities to be provided, and the utilization of centralized or multiple points of treatment facilities are required to be planned. At the last stage, after set up of treatment plant, it is required to be prepared or confirm proper operation and maintenance of the plant, this require time to time monitor of the plant.

5.2 Effluent Treatment Plant

Effluent Treatment plant is basically utilized to eliminate contaminants from wastewater. The methodologies used for the treatment is classified broadly into physical, chemical, and biological processes. Any industry required to install an effluent treatment plant (ETP) has to consider several factors, such as,

- Information about the nature and characteristics of industries wastewater is required.
- Quantity and quality of wastewater needed to be treated, etc.

This information is extracted by analyzing the samples taken from the industry in a reputed laboratory. Box 5.1 depicts the factors need to be taken into consideration while planning for effluent treatment plant (ETP).

Box 5.1 Factors to be considered for planning an ETP.

Factors to be considered for planning an ETP

- National or International standards based on which the plant is going to operate.
- Type of waste water generated from the industry
- Volume of wastewater.
- Type of chemicals present in wastewater.
- Concentration of chemicals in effluent, for instance, $35m^3$/hours, with COD of 500 mg/L, BOD of 300 mg/L, and pH of 11.5.
- Cost to be invest in constructing an ETP, that is, total budget of the plant.
- Budget allocation for running an ETP.
- Is there any planning to increase the production in future, if yes, then will this increase the quantity of effluent to be treated.
- Is land area already available or would be purchased on which the plant is going to build, and if land is needed to be purchased, then budget allocation for procurement. If it is not possible to procure large land, then Common Effluent treatment plant (CETP) can also be considered.
- ETP expert or designer is already available or needed to hire.
- Decision to be drawn on what type of plant is best suited to be built.
- Finally, the staff are trained enough to operate and maintain an ETP or they need proper training or trained staff is needed to be hire for successfully running an ETP.

5.2.1 Requirement of ETP

Effluent treatment plant is required for following reasons,

- Industrial effluent needed to be clean in order to safely discharge into water reservoir.
- In order to reduce the usage of fresh or potable water in industries.
- With the purpose of minimizing the expenditure on water procurement.
- In order to meet the quality standard set up by regulatory authorities of respective countries.
- In order to safeguard environment against pollution and thus paving way to sustainable development.

5.2.2 Design of ETP

The principle of design of ETP lies to treat non-hazardous industrial waste water and must focus on cost-effective, minimal manpower and needs minimal maintenance etc. The design and size of the ETP is influenced by numerous factors but broadly can be classified into three types, that is, the quality and quantity of the discharge effluents, land availability, and monitory considerations for construction, operation and maintenance. If enough land is not available, in that case, common effluent treatment plant (CETP) can be preferred over ETP. Box 5.2 depicts the flow chart indicating the designing of effluent treatment plant. The area dimension of the ETP depends mainly on-

- Flow rate,
- Quality of wastewater to be treated, and
- Type of biological treatment to be used.

Therefore, it is categorically clear that design of effluent treatment plant is highly influenced by industry and site. The major facts which are taken into consideration while designing effluent treatment plants are-

- Characteristics of Site in ETP design,
- Characteristics of Wastewater in ETP design, and
- Questionnaire for effluent treatment plant design.

Characteristics of Site in ETP design

ETP design requires information on the characteristics of site, such as, topology, soils, geology, climate, hydrology, and land use. It is essential to know the depth of rock layer and topography as this information assist for using gravity flow and burial of pipes. Generally in maps, the rock heights and depth are shown by different colors, usually green and yellow. Since ETP plant may affects land use in ETP construction, therefore, soil thickness, its characteristics, content, inorganic, organic matter and permeability is also recoded. When treatment of wastewater involves process of evaporation and infiltration is also a problem, in that case, precipitation and evapotranspiration is also considered.

Characteristics of Wastewater in ETP design

The characteristics of wastewater, such as, physical, chemical, and biological characters are required to be taken into consideration while designing ETP. The size of effluent treatment plant is influenced by flow rate (measured in m^3/day).

Box 5.2 Flow Chart of Design of ETP

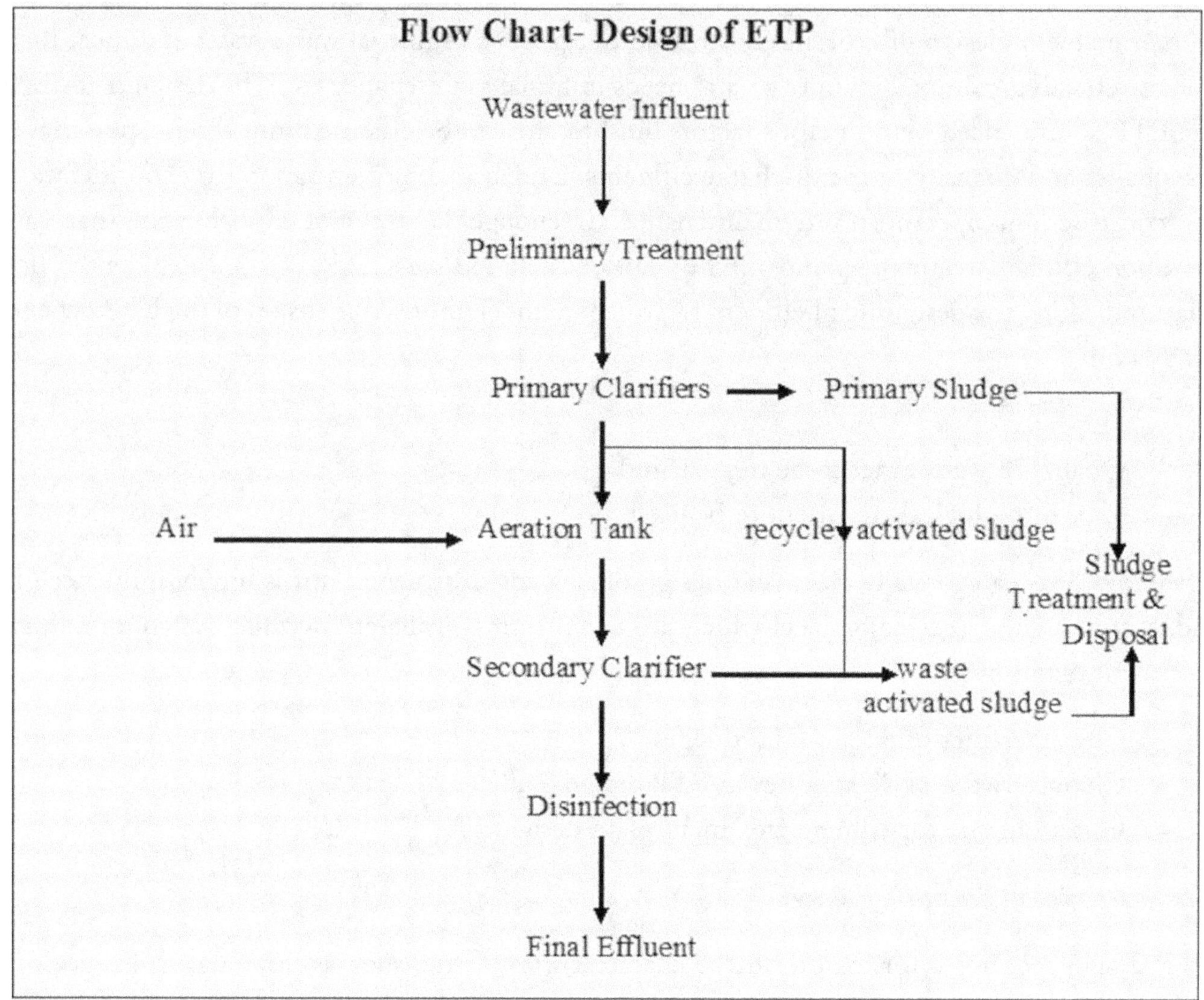

It is essential to correctly estimate the flow rate or flow of wastewater for the reason that any wrong estimation would affect hydraulic computations, channels, pipes, and equalization ponds. It should be noted that besides assisting in reducing toxicity of wastewater, equalization pond is also constructed to maintain constant flow downstream treatment process.

The physical characteristics of wastewater, such as, pH, color, turbidity, temperature, suspended solids, oil and grease etc. indicates the degree of pollution. This also ensures that the influent needed pre-treatment before discharging it into the environment. Temperature is an essential factor as high temperature influence the reaction rate by increasing it.

The chemical characteristics, such as, presence of heavy or toxic metals, organic or inorganic matters in solution or gaseous form as well as BOD and COD helps to determine the quality of effluent. Biological oxygen demand measures the quantity of biological substances present in effluent while Chemical oxygen demand checks biodegradable and non-biodegradable organics. Comparing the ratio of BOD and COD indicates the health of ETP. BOD data indicates the comparison for treated and untreated effluent, thus giving an idea about the efficiency of effluent treatment plant. It is essential to keep a check on inorganic substances, such as, nitrogen, chlorine, phosphorous, cyanides, sulphur, and heavy metals for the reason that these elements might be responsible for algae growth eventually leading to eutrophication and presence of harmful metals increases the toxicity of wastewater.

The biological characteristics, such as, the presence of E. Coli bacteria and various other saprophytic or pathogenic microbes indicates the quality of wastewater. The microbial action usually generate gases and based on the types of gases, it is easy to determine whether aerobic or anaerobic degradation is taking place.

Questionnaire for Effluent Treatment Plant Design-

The questionnaires basically assist one to design and planned effluent treatment plant in better way. The questionnaires is already discussed in last section, given in box 5.1. These question are meant to understand the type of effluent treatment plant required to be designed, operate and maintain. It prepared for the unforeseen circumstances and assist for properly monitoring all the process involves in effluent treatment plant.

5.2.3 Treatment and Mechanism of ETP

The treatment of effluent is determined based on the level of treatment they required. Broadly these are categorized into Preliminary, Primary, Secondary, and Tertiary or Advanced treatment. The mechanism of the treatment is also classified into physical, chemical, and biological, which involves a number of different process. These processes many times used together in a single treatment plant. Table 5.4 depicts the treatment and mechanism of ETP. The preliminary treatment involves the removal of large sized impurities, such as, rags, wood logs, cloths, sticks, plastics, etc. The process involves is physical process. In primary treatment, floating and settleable materials are eliminated using both physical and chemical process. The secondary treatment involves the elimination of biodegradable organic matter and suspended solids, the process used to accomplish this treatment method is basically biological and chemical process. In the last stage, that is, the tertiary treatment mainly eliminate residual suspended solids and dissolved solids and the process applied is physical, chemical, and biological, and generally refer as *Advanced Treatment.*

Table 5.4 Treatment and Mechanism of ETP

Treatment Level	Purpose	Method Involves	Process or Mechanism
Preliminary treatment	Elimination of large sized impurities such as rags, cloths, plastics, wood logs, paper, sticks, etc. that may interference with the process and damage the equipment also.	– Screening and grinding, – Equalization, and – Oil Separation.	Physical process
Primary treatment	Elimination of floating and settleable materials, such as, suspended solids and organic matter.	– Neutralization, – Coagulation, – Flocculation, – Sedimentation, and – Floatation	Physical and Chemical process
Secondary treatment	Elimination of biodegradable organic matter and suspended solids.	– Activated sludge, – Aerated lagoons, – Trickling filter, – Anaerobic lagoons, – Stabilization ponds	Biological and Chemical process
Tertiary or Advanced treatment	Elimination of residual, suspended, dissolved solids.	– Ultrafiltration, – Reverse osmosis, – Ion exchange, – Dentrification, – Coagulation, – Sedimentation.	Physical, Chemical, and Biological process.

5.2.4 ETP Plant Operations

The plant operation includes following parts-

- Screening or Screen Chamber
- Collection Tank
- Equalization tank,
- Flash Mixer,
- Clarriflocculator,
- Aeration tank,

- Clarifier,
- Sludge thickener, and
- Drying beds.

ETP plant operation starts with the elimination of relatively large solids in screen chambers. Screening is basically a filtration process for the parting of coarse particles from the influent. Stainless steel net with variable pore size is used for the process. Screens are also used to be regularly clean to avert clogging. From screen chamber, the effluent water is collected and store in collection tank, and from here it is pumps to the equalization tank. Equalization makes the waste water or effluent homogenous. The influent received in equalization tank does not have same pH all the time. The retention time in equalization tank depends upon the capacity of treatment plants which is generally 8 to 16 hours and thus helps in neutralization. It also eliminates shock loading, ultimately reducing suspended solid and total dissolved solids by the addition of coagulants.

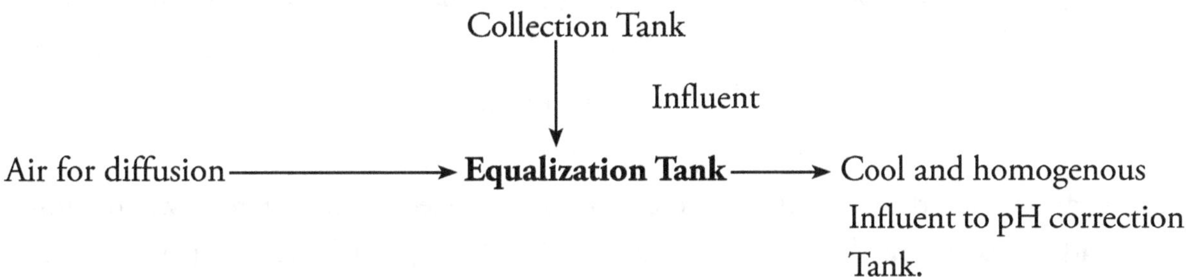

From equalization tank, effluent is pump to pH correction tank, where pH of the influent is corrected to meet the standard. As per the requirement, acid or alkali is added. For instance, lime approximately 800 to 1000 mg/L is added to correct the pH up to 8 to 9.0.

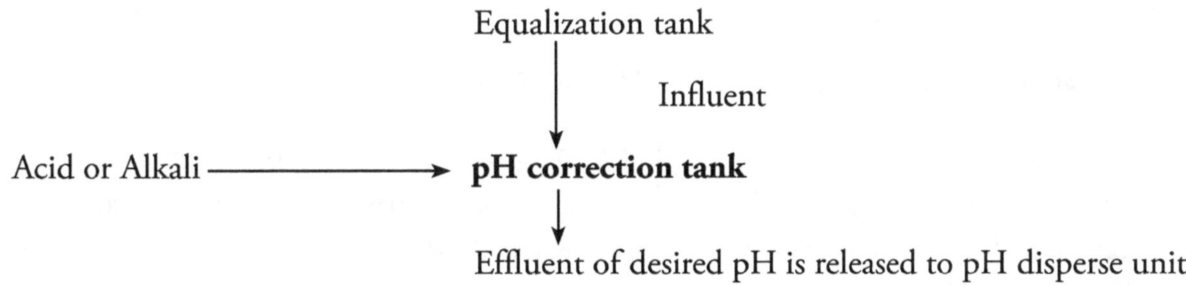

From pH correction tank, the effluent are pumped to disperse tank, where it is properly mix to provide appropriate aeration. In this, the water is circulated continuously by the stirrer and flocculants are added that assist in the slow mixing ultimately result in the formation of macro flocs, which finally settles out in the clarifier zone. The disperse tank mixes the sludge coming from recycle tank with effluent for appropriate aeration.

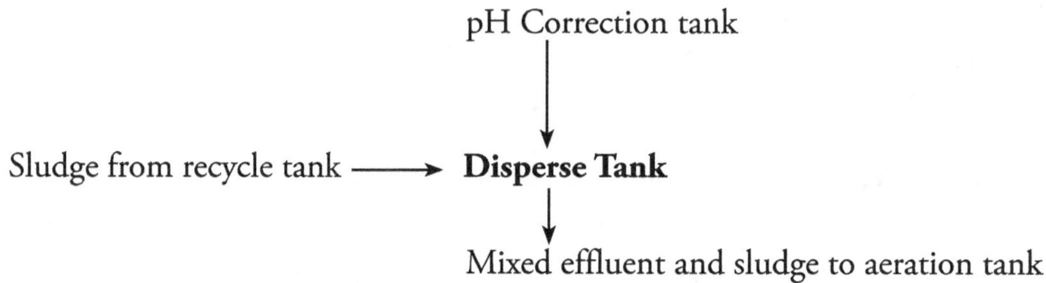

From diffuser tank, it is directed to aeration where air is blown for oxidation process and aerobic bacteria is added to stabilize and eliminate organic matter present in the effluent.

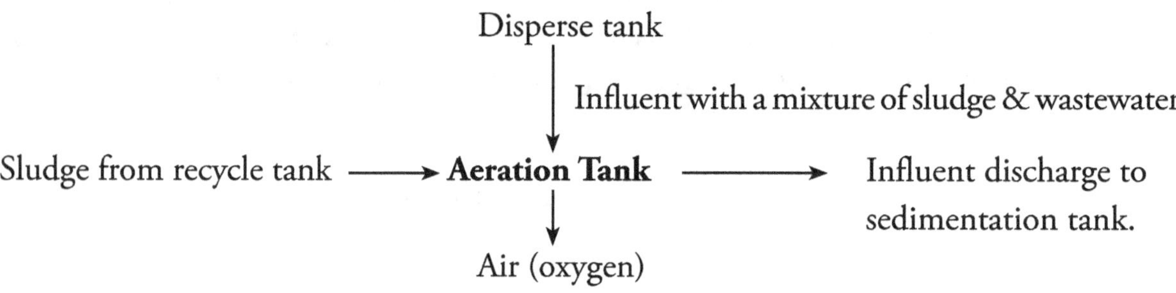

From aeration tank, the influent discharged is pumped to sedimentation tank where sludge is settled down and passed to the sludge thickening chamber. Sludge thickener received inlet effluent with 60 percent water and 40 percent solids. It is then passed through the centrifuge. In centrifugation, solid and liquid are separated. The purpose of sludge thickener is to reduce the water content to 40 percent, which is then reprocessed and then collected at the bottom. The sludge is dried and the partial amount of sludge is returned back to the aeration tank through recycle tank and disperse tank.

5.2.5 Operation and Maintenance Requirement Identification

An ETP installation required appropriate protocol or etiquette for operation and maintenance. The preparation of operation and maintenance manual needed inventory preparation at the very first stage which is written down for the proper installation by the contractor who is responsible for design and finally builds the installation. After completion of the manual, it is handover to the concerning authority for whom the installation is build.

Operation and maintenance manual would provide with the following maintenance requirement, given as below,

- Maintenance of various equipment and proper record keeping,
- Storeroom and spare parts inventory,
- Manufacturer operation and maintenance literature,

- ETP plant manager,
- ETP plant operators,
- Mechanical and Electrical Technicians,
- Laboratory analyst, and
- Labor or Helper.

ETP operation required appropriate training to execute all the task provided to them successfully. The basic aim of reliable ETP operation is 'Training needs identification, imparting training, training effectiveness evaluation and re-training.'

Training can be provided either by in-house experts, research and academic institutes, or by sending workers to professional bodies providing training. The best choice among them is to hire professional experts of ETP operating agency, as the training provided by such experts are generally energies with case-studies, practical hints, solution, and participant finds easier to communicate. This training can be provided at ETP site itself and this took approximately six to ten working days at a stretch. Orientation courses can also be provided to enhance staff competency.

5.2.6 Guidelines for Safety in ETP Operation

The safety guidelines in ETP operation involves,

- Hazard identification,
- Personnel protective equipment for ETP operation and maintenance,
- Do's and Don'ts in ETP operation for safety,
- Safe handling of Chemicals,
- Monitoring all necessary parameters time to time, and
- Guidelines for record keeping.

The operators or workers in ETP plant works indoor as well as outdoor and are exposed to various types of hazards, such as, excessive noise, unpleasant odor, or chemical agents, etc. The ETP plant operates 24 hours a day and 7 days a week. This involves exposure to a variety of hazards. Some of them are listed as below-

- Danger of burn by hot vapors or steam, solvents and other liquids, by contact with hot surface, etc.
- Electric shocks caused by contact with faulty electrical equipment, cables, etc.
- Possibility of fire and explosions due to the formation and release of flammable gases during processing.
- Acute intoxication caused by erroneous drinking of untreated waste water.
- Injuries, especially affecting or harming eyes, caused by flying particles, in particular from rotating brush cleaning or wheel grinding, etc.

The planning of Personnel protective equipment for ETP operation and maintenance requires to considered following points,

- Impact, penetration or compression when doing maintenance tasks.
- Harmful dust.
- Chemical handlings.
- Obnoxious odors of decomposing matter.
- Heat or cold and wettings.
- Oxygen deficiency.
- Light (optical) radiation.
- Electric shocks.
- Rain or storm.
- Hydrogen sulphides.
- Biological exposure from raw or treated effluents and sludge handlings.
- Noise of machines and vibrations.
- Fire extinguishers.
- First aid box, etc.

It is utmost required to carefully follow all the do's and don'ts while performing any task in ETP plants. Some of them are mentioned below,

- Wear safety shoes with non-slip soles.
- Always wear personal protective equipment to avert any sort of exposure of skin and eyes to corrosive liquid, vapors, gases, or solids.
- Without the supervision of expert, avoid mixing of chemicals.
- Properly check all equipment, especially electrical equipment before use for safety reasons.
- Obey all safety instructions regarding the storage, handlings, transport or pouring of chemicals, etc.

Corrosive chemicals are used in various types of operation and process in ETP plants. It is essential to pay attention to all rules of chemical handling, while handling all sort of corrosive chemicals during operation of ETP. For instance, chlorine is corrosive and can burn moist body surfaces, such as, eyes, throat, nose, lungs, wet skin, as chlorine forms harmful acids when it reacts with moisture. Moreover long term exposure to even low concentrations of chlorine may affect lung adversely. Therefore, there are certain guidelines to handle chlorine equipment or such corrosive chemicals, which required to be strictly followed for safety reasons.

To confirm that ETP plant is performing according to the standard and all analysis are performing accordingly, it is essential to examine certain parameters which provide guidance or hint regarding performance of ETP, such as,

- pH.
- Suspended Solids.
- Total Solids.
- Total Dissolved Solids.
- Biochemical oxygen demand (BOD).
- Chemical oxygen demand (COD).
- Dissolved oxygen (DO).
- Chlorine demand.
- Residual chlorine.
- Temperature.
- Mixed Liquor Suspended Solids (MLSS).
- Mixed Liquor Volatile Suspended Solids (MLVSS).
- Sludge Volume Index (SVI).

Besides guidelines for keeping record are also provided. Record keeping is important as this ensures that all equipment, chemicals, are properly maintained and operated.

5.3 Sewage Treatment Plant (STP)

A sewage treatment plant (STP) is basically designed to handle the quantity of sewage and has ability to deliver treated water of satisfactory quality, on a daily basis, at least for 10 to 15 years. For proper functioning, STP requires appropriate design and engineering. Various disparities exist in designing and engineering of STP due to permutations and combination of architects, builders or developers, vendors, and consultants.

The concept of sewage treatment plant is very simple which involves the conversion of untreated quantity of water into clean water by a group of microorganism. This involves the production of compact solid biomass as a by-product. However, implementing this simple concept is a difficult task and so challenging. To implement this simple principle requires complete knowledge of mechanical and chemical engineering as well as familiarity of biology of microorganisms.

5.3.1 Functions and Design of STP

The function and design of sewage treatment plant includes –

5.3.1.1 Bar Screen Chamber

5.3.1.2 Oil and Grease Trap

5.3.1.3 Equalization Tank

5.3.1.4 Raw Sewage Life Pumps

5.3.1.5 Aeration Tank

5.3.1.6 Secondary clarifiers/Settling Tanks

5.3.1.7 Sludge Recirculation

5.3.1.8 Clarified water sump

5.3.1.9 Filter feed pumps

5.3.1.10 Pressure sand filter (PSF)

5.3.1.11 Activated Carbon filter

5.3.1.12 Disinfection of treated water

5.3.1.13 Excess sludge handlings.

5.3.1.1 Bar Screen Chamber

The mechanism of bar screen involves the prevention of large sold particles into STP to avoid any sort of clogging as well as ensuring the proper functioning of STP pumps. It is also referred as bar screen channel. The design of bar screen involves the vertical bar screen, set across the sewage flow, usually having a gaps between 10 and 25 mm. A set up of bar screen depends on the size of STP, for smaller STP, single fine bar screen is appropriate but for larger STP, two bar screens are used – a coarse bar screen and a fine bar screen. It is essential to check and clean the bar screen at frequent intervals and also ensure that no large gaps should be formed because of the corrosion of the screen. Replaced unserviceable or corroded bar screen as soon as possible to ensure proper functioning.

5.3.1.2 Oil and Grease Trap

The oil and grease trap is fixed at the discharge point of the kitchen area to trap solid and fatty matter at source itself. The wastewater released from this section is then transferred to equalization tank. The solid and fatty waste which are trapped and finally separated are disposed of with other biodegradable waste, which are eventually utilized as feed for piggeries. The purpose of separating solid and fatty waste from waste water at source itself is basically to reduce the retention time of contact in order to ensure that wastewater does not absorb any additional organic pollutants due to leaching of these substances. This trap is inevitable for commercial and industrial unit with a canteen on campus, not for any residential complex. To confirm proper functioning of this trap, it is essential to check and clean trap at frequent intervals.

5.3.1.3 Equalization Tank

The sewage after primary treatment from bar screen chamber as well as oil and grease trap enters into the equalization tank. The first collection tank in STP is the equalization tank. The main function of this tank is to act as a buffer by collecting all the incoming raw sewage that comes at extensively fluctuating rates, thus equalizes the sewage and finally passing it to the rest of the STP at an average flow rates or steady flow rates. The purpose of equalization tank is to collect the incoming sewage at a high rates during the peak hours and releases them gradually during non-peak hours when there is no or little incoming sewage. Therefore, the equalization tank is applied only for buffering the daily fluctuations in the sewage flow quantity. It must be of satisfactory dimensions to handle the peak time inflow sewage volumes. The peak time and volumes are basically site specific and also variable. In residential area, the equalization tank have a capacity to handle 4 to 6 hours of average hourly flow during morning major peak hours and minimum minor peak at the late evening hours. While designing for residential area, it is essential to consider weekends hours also, because of heavier sewage generation in weekends. Whereas in commercial complexes, the maximum peak hours or flows occurs during the lunch hours and in case of manufacturing plants, the shifts timing are very crucial. The major peak hours or flow are during breakfast, lunch, and dinner in manufacturing plants. A scientific method is also given for calculating the required capacity of the equalization tank. In this process, the graph is usually plotted between the projected inflow and outflow over a 24 hours period.

For proper functioning of equalization tank, it is estimated to keep proper air mixing uniformly over the entire floor of the tank as well as placement of diffusers and the air flow rate must also be properly adjusted. To avoid overflow of equalization tank, empty the tank clearly before the expected peak load hours. It is better to manually evacuate sediments at least once in a year.

5.3.1.4 Raw Sewage Life Pumps

In order to evade deep excavations, a raw sewage life pumping stage is introduced so as to lift sewage easily to next level of the STP. This part is essentially beneficial as all downstream plants is generally placed at convenient level above ground which eventually results cost effective as well as maintenance also become easier. The pumping rate is set at a calibrated uniform flow which ensures the proper functioning of a downstream plants. The designing of raw sewage life pumping stage requires a capacity that is selected on the basis of daily average rated capacity of the STP. Generally it requires a pump that can be operated for 20 hours in a day and for large of STP, 22 hours in a day is normally considered. There are three difference categories of pump which are generally used for this purpose are-

- *Comminutor Pumps*

  It has a shredder option which solves the clogging issue by thrashing the obstacles. The drawback of this pump is that it mixes the non-biodegradable waste in sewage in such a way that it become impossible to separate them, eventually becomes a danger to environment.

- *Non-Clog, Solid Handling (NC-SH) Pumps*

  It has open impellers and it is the most correct choice. Failure rate of this pumps is least reported. It can handle or hold solids up to even 20 mm size. It is cost effective and repair or servicing costs is negligible. It may be serviced at the site itself within a few hours with readily or freely available spares and consumables. This pumps are also equipped with a Non Return Flap Valve in the body itself, which allows it to function as a normal foot valve, therefore priming of these pumps are not required at every point of start.

For the proper functioning of raw sewage lift pumps, it is essential to switch between the main and stand by pump at every 4 hours and always have safety guard in its proper position.

5.3.1.5 Aeration Tank

The aeration tank lies at the heart of the treatment system. The main function of the aeration tank involves the maintenance of a high population level of microbes. This mixture is referred as MLSS, that is, Mixed Liquor Suspended Solids. The Mixed Liquor when enters into clarifier tank, the microbes present in it settled at the bottom. This settled microbes are further recycled back to the aeration tank. Thus the retention period remains longer within the system. For proper functioning of aeration tank, it is essential to know the quantity of sewage to be handled per day. This estimation clarify the quantity of food available per day for the microbes, that is, Food to Microorganism Ratio(F/M ratio).These estimation are essential to extract the exact volume required for aeration tank. Further, to keep the microbes in active position, it is required to compute the quantity of air to be pumped into the aeration tank. The quantity of air required for respiration of the microbes is always higher in comparison to the quantity of air needed to keep the tanks content completely mixed. The thumb rule of aeration tank is 50–60 m³ per hours of air for every kg of BOD removed. Therefore, the design of aeration tank required the proper information of-

- The volume (size)
- Concentration of microbes to be maintained, and
- The quantity of air to be supplied per hours.

The aeration tank is usually made up of waterproof RCC construction. Operation consideration involves the maintenance of the correct design level of MLSS in the aeration tank. If there is imbalance arises in case of shortage or excess of biomass, it causes failure of the process.

5.3.1.6 Secondary Clarifier or Settling Tank

The main function of secondary clarifier or settling tank is to allow the settlement of biomass solids in the mixed liquor generating from aeration tank to the bottom of the clarifier, which thickens the settled biomass so that it produces a thick underflow and also generates clear supernatant water. This is only considered as a passive device. In the secondary clarifier all the process works under gravity. The thick biomass, finally generated, is recirculated again back to the aeration tank. The secondary clarifier or settling tank is categorized into two parts-

– *Mechanized Clarifier*
  In this, bottom of the mechanized clarifier tanks shaped as a gentle slope towards the center. The sludge settlement takes places uniformly across the floor of the tank. It has a rotating rubber blades that gradually sweep the sludge into a hopper at the center of the tank.
– *Unmechanized Clarifier*
  In this, the bottom of the tank has a steep slopes, like funnel. The sludge that enters gradually settles towards bottom and slides down the slope to accumulate at the lowest point of the funnel shaped bottom. The design of unmechanized clarifier tank usually have three categories that depends in the way in which the sludge is accumulated and returned back to the aeration tank.

Theoretically in secondary clarifier the depth has no role. Increasing depth of the clarifier assist merely in the thickening function.

5.3.1.7 Sludge Recirculation

In order to produce desired satisfactorily or high level of treatment, it is essential to run aeration tank, secondary clarifier and sludge recirculation in unanimity. These three, that is, aeration tank, secondary clarifier or settling tank and sludge recirculation, together in combination establish an activated sludge biological treatment system. To maintain high level of microbes in the aeration tank and retaining microbes at least for 25 to 30 days, the sludge recirculated from the secondary clarifier and at regular intervals the excess of microbes are taken out from the system. For instances, if total biomass present in the system is 100 kg and wasting rate is 4 kg, in this case the average age of biomass in the system is 25 days. The sludge recirculation rates are usually from 50 to 100 percent of the all the way through rate of sewage in the STP. The engineering principle is similar for both the raw sewage lift pumps as well as sludge recirculation pumps. For uninterrupted functioning of sludge recirculation it is essential to maintain the water level between the aeration tank and secondary clarifier, that is, the difference of water level between both must not be excessive or else the pump could not be able to lift the sludge and consequently the recirculation of sludge will stop.

5.3.1.8 Clarified Water Sump

The water which overflow from the secondary clarifier are collected in an intermediate clarified water sump. This zone act as a buffer tank between the secondary and tertiary treatment phases in STP. At this stage, the water quality is satisfied enough to be used for watering lawns, gardens with sufficient disinfection. This process also evade any sort of overload to the tertiary treatment process. This water can also be used for backwash purposes. The clarified water sump tank has only a passive role in STP functioning, therefore, no special requirement is needed.

5.3.1.9 Filter Feed Pump

The purpose of function of filter feed pump is to collect water from the clarified water sump and then transfer it to the pressure sand filter and activated carbon filter installed in series.

5.3.1.10 Pressure Sand Filter

The purpose of pressure sand filter is to trap the trace quantity of solids and handle in an economical manner. This is utilized as a tertiary treatment phase and can handle up to 50 mg/litre of solid. It is essentially a pressure vessel which is filled with graded media, that is, either sand or gravel. The sand applied in pressure sand filter has specific particle size which is achieved through proper sieving. The gravel layer basically gives physical support to the upper sand layer. The upper sand layer actually perform the filtration system.

5.3.1.11 Activated Carbon Filter

The purpose of activated carbon filter is to obtain the water which is already filtered by pressure sand filter. The water which activated carbon filter receives are further treated to improve the quality parameters of water especially BOD, COD, color, odor, and turbidity. The activated carbon filter is also considered as a part of tertiary treatment system, just like pressure sand filter. It is made up of either coconut shell or charcoal, making the activation process highly porous utilizing material with a large surface area. The water which are filtered by pressure sand filter are transferred to activated carbon filter for further purification.

5.3.1.12 Disinfection of treated water

At this stage, the water are further treated for disinfection to destroy all the pathogenic microorganism. The common methodologies applied for disinfection purposes are ozonisation, chlorination, and UV radiation. Among this chlorination is most common and cost effective. It is easy to handle and being safe, the common chlorine used is sodium hypochlorite at 10 to 12 percent strength.

5.3.1.13 Excess Sludge Handling

For the proper and uninterrupted functioning of STP, it is essential to take out excess of sludge from the system and disposed of satisfactorily. For this purpose five stages are involved-

- Sludge Removal
- Collection or Storage
- Conditioning
- Dewatering
- Disposal

The excess of sludge is removed from the system through the sludge recirculation pipelines, which is usually in the form of slurry. This is usually collected or accumulated into a sludge holding tank and retained under aeration tank while waiting for the dewatering operation functioning. Before starting dewatering operation, the sludge is conditioned by adding polymer or other chemicals, in order to facilitate the process. After this stage, the sludge is finally dewatered in a sludge bag or centrifuge to drain out excess of water. The sludge is poured in sludge bags, just like tea strainer the water drains out and finally the sludge collected from this process is successfully disposed of.

CHAPTER VI

Water Management

"Drops and Drops make an Ocean"

– Anonymous

6.1 Introduction

The world is already facing a problem of water stress. In today's scenario, a line from the poem of John Bunyan matches a reality, that says,

"Water water everywhere, all the world to sink.
Water water everywhere not a drop to drink"

These lines perfectly picture the requirement of water management. There is much water all around the world, but it is not fit for drinking.

There are several reasons for water scarcity but the prominent reasons may be-

- Increasing population,
- Increasing pollution and environmental issues, such as, global warming etc.,
- Rapid industrialization and urbanization,
- Delay in completing ongoing water projects,
- Uneven distribution of rainfall.
- Establishment of high water consuming industries in areas of low rainfall.

The traditional water resources are drying up due to high temperature, increase in consumption of water, and neglecting natural water reservoirs. Water Management refers to the efficient and appropriate arrangement of the hydrosphere to avoid any sort of water crisis.

Rapid industrialization and urbanization has emphasis the requirement of water management to avoid water scarcity in future. India has a long history and tradition of water harvesting, but the concept of water harvesting gradually diminishes as the time passes. Water management has seen two major shifts over the last 150 years, not only in India but worldwide and these are as follows,

- Communities and Individuals gets completely dependent on state for water and give up their own participation.
- The simple ways, such as, using raindrop has declined and more emphasis were given to dams and tubewells, as a consequences, exploitation of groundwater and rivers has drastically increases.

The importance of water management recognizes whenever country faces severe drought. Latest in 2016, approximately 330 million people were influenced by drought in India. The result was severe water shortages and desperately poor farmers suffer crop losses in Uttar Pradesh, Madhya Pradesh, Chhattisgarh, Maharashtra, Telangana, Andhra Pradesh, Karnataka, and Orissa. In Maharashtra, out of 36 district, 21 faces severe drought. Out of 51 district, 46 were hit by drought in Madhya Pradesh and 12 district of Orissa, all district except two in Telangana, at least 19, out of 33 district in Rajasthan, Out of 24, 22 district in Jharkhand, 50 district out of 75 district in Uttar Pradesh, at least 27, out of 30 district in Karnataka, were severely hit by drought. Once the crisis starts, government took some steps to provide water at drought hit regions by water tankers, even by water trains.

But this crisis would not happen if water management has done by communities, individuals, and government at right time and at right place. At today's scenario it is needed to have integrated water resources management (IWRM) or in simple term Water Management. This involves the supply of water in both quality and quantity plus the demand of water by domestic, industries, agriculture, etc. Therefore, it is, Box 6.1 indicates the relationship between supply and demand.

Box 6.1 Relationship between Supply and Demand

Supply   +   Demand ⟶ Water Management or IWRM
(Quality &   (Domestic,
Quantity   industries, or
Of water)   agriculture, etc.)

Water management can optimally be done broadly through three categories, as follows,

- Optimal application of available water resources,
- Effective demand management, and
- Prevention and control of wastage of water.

6.2 Need of Water Management

Water management is the foremost step towards economic development and poverty reduction. This can be understood by the lines of John F. Kennedy-

"Anyone who can solve the problems of water will be worthy of two Nobel prizes – one for peace and one for science."

The world population is increasing at alarming rates to almost ten billion by year 2050, and will needed more energy and safe drinking water. Global water demand is estimated to upsurge, due to excessive demand of domestic water, manufacturing and process in industries, by about 55 percent reported by Asian Development Bank Outlook Report-2016 (ADBO-2016). It is projected that by year 2050, Asia and Pacific region's more than sixty percent of population will be migrating to cities and at present Asia alone is home to 13 of the world's 22 megacities and it is expected to upsurge to 20 megacities by year 2025. In spite of this fact, approximately 1.7 billion population still lack safe drinking water and basic sanitation facilities. Moreover 80 percent of wastewater and more than 95 percent in developing countries, being discharged without primary treatment. The Report of ADBO (2016) gives a statistical report of approximately how much wastewater treated before discharging into water body. Some of them are given below-

Viet Nam – 4 percent; India – 9 percent; Philippines – 10 percent; and Indonesia – 14 percent.

Groundwater globally exploited mostly for domestic water supply, and approximately 25 to 40 percent of drinking water comes from groundwater. Asia and Pacific region alone host 7 of the world's 15 biggest extractor of groundwater. It is projected by International Institute for Applied System Analyst that in India, the People's Republic of China, and Pakistan, exploitation of groundwater will increase by 30 percent accounting for 86 percent of total groundwater extraction. This excessive extraction has drastically reduce the water table. Moreover the unhygienic environment around hand pumps, tubewells, etc. has also pollute groundwater. This has immensely increases the water quality related health disaster. The country wise detail of extraction of groundwater and their application in percentage as per 2010 report, is given in Table 6.1.

Table 6.1 Annual Groundwater Extraction by Countries as per 2010 Report.

Country	Annual Groundwater Extraction (Km^3/year)	Percentage (%) of Groundwater Extraction for –		
		Irrigation Use	Domestic Use	Industry Use
India	251	89	9	2
China	111.95	54	20	26
United States	111.70	71	23	6
Pakistan	64.82	94	6	0

(Cont.)

Country	Annual Groundwater Extraction (Km³/year)	Percentage (%) of Groundwater Extraction for –		
		Irrigation Use	Domestic Use	Industry Use
Iran	63.40	87	11	2
Bangladesh	30.21	86	13	1
Saudi Arabia	24.24	92	5	3
Indonesia	14.93	2	93	5
Russian federation	11.62	3	79	18
Syria	11.29	90	5	5
Japan	10.94	23	29	48
Thailand	10.74	14	60	26
Italy	10.40	67	23	10

(Source: Asian Water Development Outlook Report 2016).

It is estimated by Global Water Partnership (GWP) and Organization of Economic Cooperation and Development (OCED) that water insecurity cost the global economy approximately 500 million dollar annually. Moreover it is a total slog on the world economy of one percent or more of global gross domestic product (GDP). Asia and Pacific region are estimated as a major global hot spot for water insecurity or water stress. The projection given by International Institute for Applied Systems Analysis suggest that approximately 3.4 billion population will be living in water stressed area of Asia by year 2050, in their report 'Asia Water Future and Solution 2050.' The worst hit area which will have lowest per capita water availability will be Afghanistan, China, India, Singapore, and Pakistan.

Further, Intergovernmental Panel on Climate Change (IPCC) fifth assessment report quantified that Climate change over the twenty first century is projected to decrease renewable groundwater and surface water resources significantly in most of the subtropical region which eventually exaggerate the competition for water among stakeholders. The Report of Massachusetts Institute of Technology estimated that population growth and industrialization, coupled with Climate Change has greater impact on water security. This has intensify the water insecurity as well as water stressed region worldwide, in their report on 'Climate Change Projection and Water Security.'

World Research Institute (WRI) scored and ranked future water stress countries using a collaborative of Climate Models and Socioeconomic Scenarios. They quantified 167 countries on the basis of water stress by year 2020, 2030, and 2040. As per their estimation thirty three countries will be facing extreme water stress in 2040. Among thirty three countries, fourteen alone will be in Middle East, and moreover Chile, Estonia, Namibia, and Botswana will be significantly highly water stressed countries by year 2040. In Middle East Countries, Kuwait, Palestine, Bahrain, Qatar, Israel, Oman, Saudi Arabia, United Arab Emirates, and Lebanon is already highly dependent on desalinated sea water and groundwater, and it is considered to be least water secure country in the world, the projection made by WRI suggest that the situation for these middle east countries is only going to be worst, and this will only worsen the situation by setting great challenge to deal with water security.

This made essential to secure water resources and use it efficiently and sustainably to make it available for future generation. The world has agreed and stressed on 'Integrated Water Resource Management (IWRM)' for protecting natural water resources. There are several ways to manage and conserve water resources. The objective of Water supply management is to improve the supply by minimizing losses and wastage and unaccounted water in the transmission main and distribution system. This Chapter discusses some of the prominent methodologies to conserve and manage water resources, such as, rainwater harvesting, reuse and recycling of wastewater, efficient management of water in agriculture, industries, and at domestic level.

6.2.1 Climate Change and Water Scarcity

Climate change, now a days, a very common phrase and we generally make climate change responsible for all our miseries, be it extreme hot, cold, flood, drought, disease, etc. But are we really doing justice by blaming 'Climate Change' for all our problems? To understand this, let us see, what is climate change? Climate change is generally refers as the rise in average surface temperature on earth, but is it right to say? No, not actually. Climate Change is basically the change in average condition of particular place over a long period of time. But then what is global warming? Is it synonymous of climate change? Actually, there is a fine difference between global warming and climate change. Global warming is a rise in average surface temperature on earth and Climate change refers to all changing factors of earth's climate including temperature, rain, wind, humidity, atmospheric gases, so temperature is not only thing that is changing and it is not just getting hotter. Here, we can say global warming is a specific term used to indicate climate change & climate changes includes global warming. Earth's climate is not constant, it's changing and since ~ 1800, the average global surface temperature has risen by about one degree celsius.

There are so many reasons for climate change – natural and anthropogenic. The one prominent natural cause is the earth's changes in the axis which includes variation of earth's tilt, variation of earth's orbit, and wobble of earth's axis, these three types of cycle also affects climate in the long term. The prominent artificial cause is the Green House Gases (GHG), which eventually leads to Green House Effect (GHE). Though greenhouse effect is a natural phenomenon which is essential for the existence of life on earth, but it is a manmade greenhouse gases that exacerbate the whole process resulting in climate change. The global warming potential is the relative ability of one molecule of a given greenhouse gas to contribute to global warming.

The impacts of climate change, this includes, variability in rainfall, increasing sea level, variation in season length, longer summer, and shorter winter. How serious is climate change? Climate change is serious as it is projected that by year 2080, that approximately 1000 million people will be at risk of hunger and coastal flooding, and more than 3000 million people will be at risk of water shortage and malaria, if the temperature exceeds above 1.5 °C (as per Global Environment Change report). Figure 6.1 indicates the seriousness of climate change or millions at risk, extracted from the report of 'Global Environment Change.'

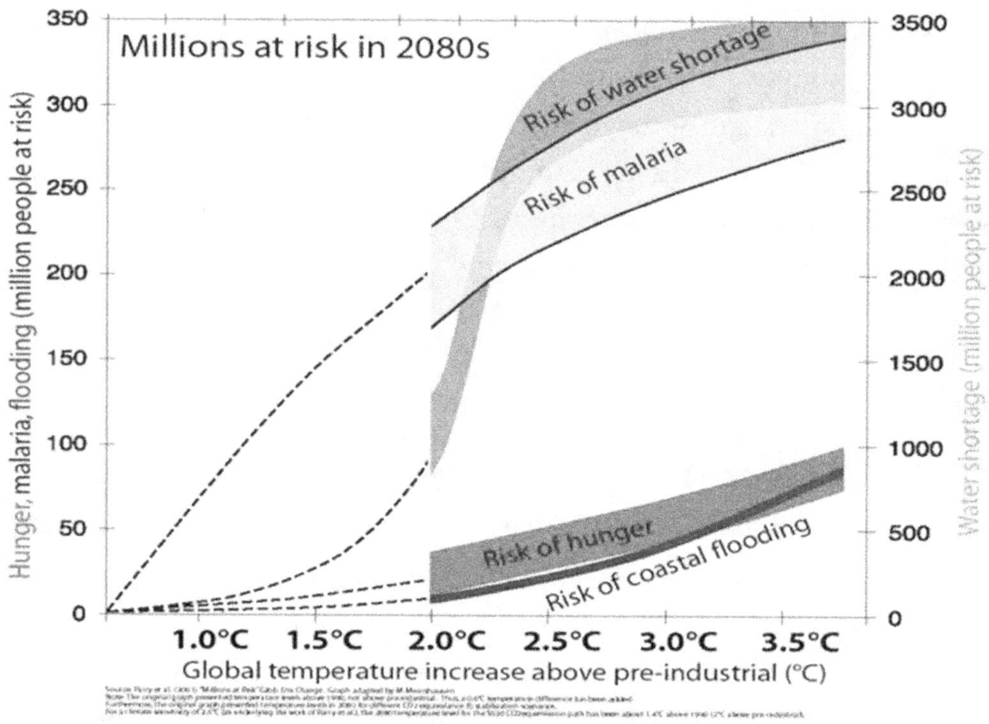

Figure 6.1 Seriousness of climate change impact

(Source: Global Environment Change Report)

Over and all, the climate related hazards includes river basin flooding, flash flood, avalanche, wild land fires, haze, tropical cyclones, ice storms, hail and lightning, drought, heavy precipitations, etc. Who is at Risk? Mostly the poorest people, inhabitants of coastal town, villages, hill communities, fisherman hamlets, islanders, farming communities, and megacities with high water demand. What is the impact of climate change on water? It is estimated by Michel and Pandya, (2009) that water accessibility per capita declines by almost 70 percent since 1950, and projected that by 2025, most of the region will be facing either physical or economic scarcity of water. When we say physical or economic scarcity of water, it means when human, institutional, and financial capital limit access to water resources even though they are naturally available in plenty. Further, according to IPCC, more than 90 percent probability is there that most river basin are likely to become drier which eventually leads to persistent water shortage. Moreover, International Alert reported that there are 46 countries where climate change and water related crisis create a high risk of violent conflicts and this includes India, Bangladesh, and Pakistan also. This justify the statement given by Ban Ki Moon UN Secretary General (2008)-"*A shortage of water resources could spell increase conflicts in the future.*" Some experts asserts that in the near future just like gold and oil, water will also become one of the precious commodity, and further, wars will be fought over 'who owns the water supply.' As a result of climate change, intensified water scarcity has consequences not only for the regions socioeconomic development and the war against poverty, but also for its overall peace and political stability. The South Asian region (which includes Afghanistan, India, Pakistan, Bhutan, Bangladesh, Nepal, Maldives, and SriLanka) shares a common water resources and usage pattern and therefore shares a common water management challenges also.

How we could response to climate change? There are two approaches – mitigation & adaptation, and we need to integrate both of these. Mitigation refers to the involvement of any artificial element that can either decrease the source of GHG emission (abatement) or enhance their sinks (sequestration), while adaptation refers to the degree to which adjustments are possible in practice, processes or structure of systems to projected or actual change of climate. Actually, adapting to climate change is neither a 'one-time activity' nor it is a 'one-size-fits-all' approach to manage climate change impacts.

Let us now focus on our lifestyle – On an average water footprint of 100gm of chocolate bar is 2400 liters and water footprint of milk powder is 4600 liters/kg. Therefore the composition of dark chocolate involves 40 percent cocoa paste, where water footprint is 33260 litre per kg; 20 percent cocoa butter, where water footprint is 50730 litre per kg; and 40 percent sugar, where water foot print is 1526 litre per kg. The computation of the composition of dark chocolate, that is, 40 percent of 33260 plus 20 of percent 50730 plus 40 percent of 1526 gives 2,40,60 litre per kg. This means for one 100 gram of dark chocolate bar, water footprint is 2400 litre. Since the water footprint of milk powder is 4600 litre per kg, therefore milk chocolate will have a bit larger water footprint in comparison to dark chocolates, that is, approximately, 2500 litre for one 100 gram milk chocolate bar, when total cocoa content remains the same. The cocoa paste and cocoa butter content is the most decisive for water footprint. Drinking tea or coffee, what saves a water more? Let us find out. To make a standard cup of coffee, one need to have 7 gram of roasted coffee, and it is estimated that it costs approximately 21,000 litre of water to generate one kg of roasted coffee. Therefore, a water footprint of standard cup of coffee is 140 litre. If a standard cup of coffee is 125 ml, one required more than 1100 drops of water for generating one drop of coffee. Whereas, a standard cup of tea, say of 250 ml, required only 30 litre of water, which suggest drinking tea would saves a lot of water than drinking coffee. Similarly it costs 2700 liters of water to make one cotton t-shirt. Globally, the annual cotton production evaporates 210 billion cubic meters of water and pollutes 50 billion cubic meters (BCM) of water. This is 3.5 percent of the global water use for crop production. (*Source – Indian Institute of Public Administration, New Delhi, India, 2017*).

We seriously need water management or IWRM (Integrated water resource management), which can be achieved only if we could able to balance supply and demand of water. There are various methods for water management such as rainwater or water harvesting, at industries, domestic, agriculture, and at personnel level, which will be discussed further in this chapter.

What we can do to save water at our own? –by changing our lifestyle. Changing our attitudes means modifying the way we think and the way we see and perceive things. This we can achieve through increasing knowledge and raising awareness. It means developing values which implies practicing ethical actions that improves the relationship between and amongst individual and their environment. We also need to adopt patterns of productions, consumptions, & reproduction that safeguard earth's regenerative capacities, human rights and community well-being.

6.3 Rainwater Harvesting

India is one of the most gifted nation in the world in terms of average rainfall, approximately precipitation is 105 cm per year. Maximum rainfall of the world is in India. Total rainfall, approximately 90 percent, is in 90 days or 90 hours. Water is enough, the only need is to manage the available water resources properly. Though climate change or global warming has influenced the water resources, recharging capacity has also gradually declined but harvesting rainwater is one of the simplest solution to overcome these problems. Artificial recharging can solve the ground water crisis as it assist in protecting the water resources and assures a constant supply of clean water.

India's rainfall is influenced by monsoon, which is unpredictable. Recognizing this fact, water harvesting was adopted in India, more than 150 years ago and is passed down from generation to generation, which has now been lost. Water harvesting was conducted in variety of ways, such as,

- Raindrop were harvested directly. From rooftops, water was collected and stored it in tanks built in courtyards. From open community lands, raindrops were collected and stored it in artificial wells.
- Runoff water was harvested by capturing water from swollen streams during the monsoon season and finally these are stored. Such stored water were referred in different parts of India as *'ahars'* in Bihar, *'zings'* (small tanks fed by runoff from melting glaciers) in Ladakh, *'johads'* in Rajasthan, *'eris'* in Tamilnadu, and *'jheel'* in Gujarat and so on.
- The excess water was harvested from flooded rivers in places like West Bengal and in North Bihar.

Rainwater harvesting is a promising technology, and it has been recorded that in India the potential of rain water harvesting is enormous and unquestionable. If adopting traditional ways of harvesting rainwater is applied during normal rainfall, it would help to recharge the depleting groundwater and stored water which can be used in irrigation during water crisis. This rainwater harvesting can also increases the productivity of the rainfed lands.

Rainwater harvesting is capable of providing drinking water even in the worst of drought situation and is also the most efficient method to collect water, if rain water harvesting projects are handled and implemented well. The cases of Dematwelhinna in SriLanka and in Ralegaon Siddhi, Sukhomajri and several villages in Alwar district in India has clearly shown that rainwater harvesting is given a sense of water security, eradicate poverty, reduced health risks, decrease distress migration and increased income earnings opportunities by generating rural employment. Moreover, the proper implementation of rain water harvesting in these areas has been a proof that it can be used in most arid areas of South Asia to reduce vulnerability to drought.

6.3.1 Methods of Rainwater harvesting

There are several ways by which rainwater can be harvest. Generally these can be classified into two broad categories of,

6.3.1.1 Surface Runoff harvesting, and

6.3.1.2 Roof top rainwater harvesting.

6.3.1.1 Surface Runoff Harvesting

The amount of water remaining after losses due to evaporation, transpiration and percolation, etc. on the surface is known as *surface runoff*. Naturally it forms the sources for all surface water, such as, river, lakes, ponds, etc. Generally in urban areas, due to lack of proper drainage rainwater flows away as surface runoff. This runoff could be collected and applied for recharging aquifers by adopting appropriate methodologies.

6.3.1.2 Roof top rainwater harvesting

This system justify the concept to save even a single drop of rain and it catches water where it falls. In this system, roof becomes the catchment and involves the collection of water from the roof or terrace of the house or buildings. The collected water can be stored either in the tank or diverted to artificial recharge system.

Water mostly waste which falls on roof or terrace of the house or building so by trapping each drop of water, this methodology assist in supplementing the groundwater level of the area and it is also cost effective and efficient simple technology. This system involves simple components for designing roof top rainwater harvesting.

The components are as follows,

- Catchments,
- Transportation,

- First flush, and
- Filter.

Catchments-

The catchment area refers to the surface which receives rainfall directly. This can be courtyard, terrace, paved or unpaved open ground. The balcony or terrace can be a flat stone or sloping roof which receives rainwater and can contribute to the harvesting system.

Transportation-

To transfer water collected on roof is carried down to storage or harvesting system through water pipes or drains. The water pipes which are generally used should be of good quality, mostly UV resistant of required capacity can transfer water successfully. At terrace, to avoid floating of mat or any other particle with water, it is good to have wire mesh at the mouth of each drain or pipe used for transporting water to storage tank or harvesting system.

First Flush-

It is a device which is used to flush off water received in first shower. The first shower of rain water is required to be flushed off to evade any sort of contamination of the atmosphere as well as the catchment area. This device assist to eliminate even the silt or any other material deposited on roof during dry season. It is good to provide 'first rain separator' at outlet of each drainpipe.

Filter-

The general reason given to avoid or skepticism regarding recharging groundwater through rainwater harvesting, is the chance of contaminating groundwater. Therefore, appropriate filter can overcome the fear of contamination. Besides underground sewer drains should also be of good quality and should not leak or punctured. Filters generally applied eliminate microorganism, turbidity, color, etc. After first flushing of rainwater, water must be passed through appropriate filters.

Filter usually made up of sand, gravel, and nelton mesh is designed and laid on top of the storage tank. The filter assist in keeping water clean in the storage tank. As it eliminate silt, leaves, dust, and other organic matter from entering the storage tank. After every rainfall, filter should be clean to improve its efficiency. Clogged filter will hindered the process and it easily overflows. Therefore, the sand and gravel media must be taken out and washed properly after rainfall, and replaced it in filter properly. There are several types of filter are available to purify water, such as,

- Sand Gravel Filter,
- PVC-Pipe filter,
- Charcoal Filter, and
- Sponge Filter.

6.3.1.3 Methods to apply Rooftop Rainwater Harvesting-

There are several methodologies to apply rooftop rainwater harvesting. Generally it is classified into two types-

- Storage of Direct Use,
- Recharging Ground Aquifers, such as,

    - Recharging of bore wells,
    - Recharging of dug wells,
    - Recharge pits,
    - Recharge Trenches,
    - Recharge shafts or soakaways,
    - Percolation Tanks.

The system of rainwater harvesting is given in flowchart in Box 6.2

Box 6.2 System of Rainwater harvesting

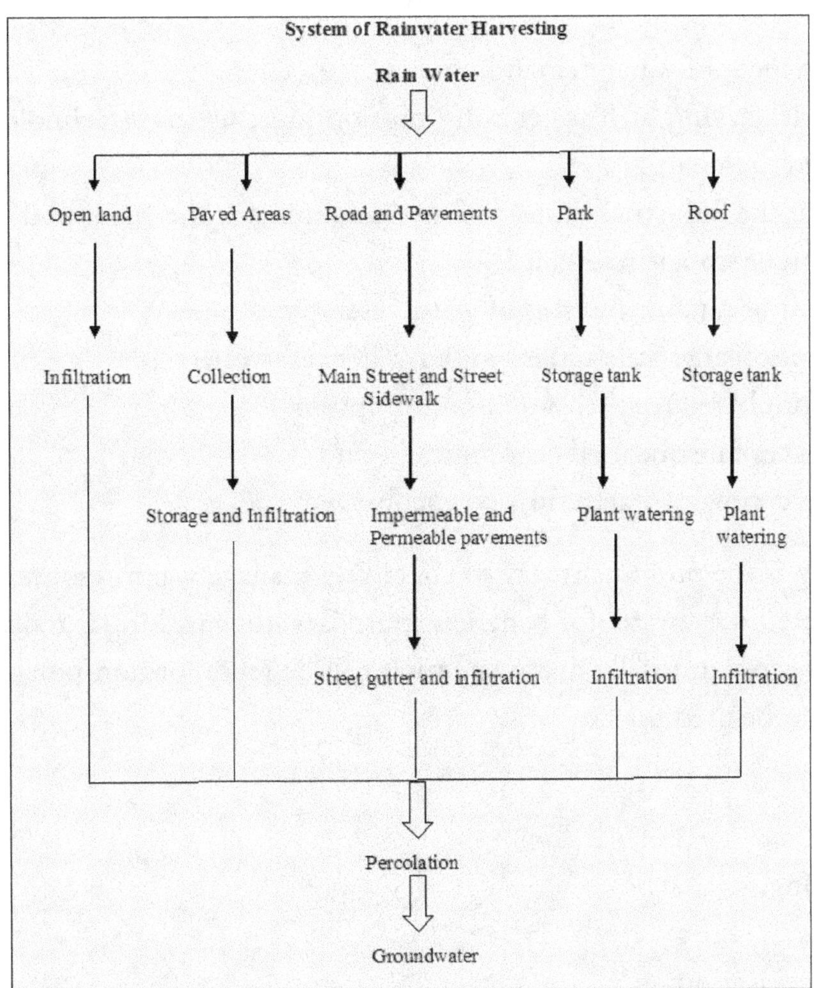

(Source: Ministry of Environment, Forest, and Climate Change, Government of India)

The potential areas where rainwater harvesting can be applied are,

- Those areas where ground water level are diminishing alarmingly.
- Due to rapid industrialization and urbanization, the infiltration rate has declined drastically.
- Availability of ground water is inadequate, and
- The significant quantity of aquifer has been de-saturated.

6.4 Water Management for Industrial Waste and Municipal Sewage waste.

Industries used large quantities of water for several purposes, such as, washing, cooling, boiler feed, etc. It is required that most of the industries have poor quality of water management system, in fact, water is the most negligible part in the industries. As per principle, it is essential to assess the quantity and quality of water at both inlets and outlets of several units which is not always taken into consideration by most of the industries. Industries and Municipalities can save their future drinking water as well as conserve water throughout their production process. The efforts which can be applied for effective water management are-

- Proper assessment of water demand,
- The industries having high water consumption must use new technologies for decreasing the water requirement,
- Treatment of the industrial wastes before discharging in the water bodies,
- Construction of storage reservoir,
- Improvement of catchment areas of water reservoir,
- Development of large scale underground water reservoir,
- Industries should reduce their water consumption,
- Water resources must be used economically, and
- Reuse and recycling of water must be encouraged.

Reuse and recycling is the prominent way to effectively manage water resources. Water Recycling means to reuse treated wastewater for beneficial purposes, thus making it more cost effective and also protecting water resources. Treated wastewater can be reuse for non-potable purposes. Other than drinking, it can be used for-

- Agriculture,
- Landscape,
- Toilet flushing,
- Public Parks,
- Golf course irrigation,

- Dust control,
- Artificial lakes,
- Concrete mixing,
- Construction activities,
- Cooling water for power plants and oil refineries, and
- Processing water for plants, mills, etc.

Recycled water that meet up all the standards, criteria, and regulation of water are safe to use for non-potable purposes as no human health problems arises or documented hitherto, due to recycled water. Earth itself reuses and recycled water naturally for millions of years through hydrological cycle or water cycle. Water recycling is based on the phenomenon of hydrological cycle and speed up the process. It is often characterized by –

- Planned, and
- Unplanned water recycling.

Planned water recycling refers to those that are generated with an aim of beneficially reusing a recycled water supply.

Unplanned water recycling involves where cities withdraw their water supplies from rivers, and water is treated, reused, and piped into the water supply a number of times before the last downstream user draw the water.

Recycled water can efficiently assist in developing water security among stakeholders as long as it is properly treated to confirm water quality suitable for the use. '*Gray water*' is also refers as recycled water. Basically gray water is reusable waste water from commercial, residential and industrial bathroom sinks, cloths washings drains, bath tub, shower drains, etc. Gray water can be used mostly for landscape irrigation. For developing proper standards, rules and regulation to use gray water, National Science Foundation (NSF) International has setup 'Wastewater Treatment Task.' They have come up with a new standard –'NSF 350-Onsite Residential and Commercial Reuse Treatment Systems.' However, still there are certain areas which required extensive research to drawn a conclusion, and in this view EPA and CDC brought together agency and academic experts to explore high-priority areas of Gray water, such as,

- Risk management options for Gray water,
- Exposure Risk to human and Ecosystem,
- Water scarcity, and
- Trends in water use.

Gray water has ability to meet up to 50 percent of water demand by supplying water for landscape irrigation. This can save fresh potable water for other non-potable uses, also reduces the volume of wastewater going to septic system as well as wastewater treatment plants. Besides it also upsurge the infrastructure capacity for new users. Box 6.2 depicts the application of treated water at each stages of treatment plant as per EPA (2012).

Box 6.3 Recommended water recycling and application

Recommended Water Recycling and Application	
Treatment	**Suggested Application**
Primary Treatment (Sedimentation)	No application suggested at primary level.
Secondary Treatment (Biological Oxidation, and Disinfection)	– Non-food crop irrigation, – Surface Irrigation of orchards and vineyards, – Groundwater recharge of non-potable aquifer, – Industrial cooling processes, and – Wetlands, wildlife habitat, stream augmentation.
Tertiary Treatment (Chemical coagulation, Disinfection, and Filtration)	– Toilet Flushing, – Landscape and Golf course irrigation, – Commercial uses, such as, vehicle washings, laundry facilities and window washing, etc. – Unrestricted recreational impoundment, – Food crop irrigation
After all treatments	– Groundwater recharge of potable aquifer, – Surface water recharge. – Create or Enhance Wetlands and Riparian habitats.

(Source: http://www3.epa.gov/region9/water/recycling)

6.4.1 Environmental benefits of Water Recycling

Water Recycling is responsible for remarkable environmental benefits. It provides additional sources of water which not only save fresh potable water but also decrease the diversion of water from sensitive ecosystem. It also reduce wastewater discharge into water body, and thus prevent pollution, and protect water resources. Recycled water can also be used either for enhancing or for creating wetlands and riparian habitats.

6.4.1.1 Reduce diversion of Fresh water from sensitive ecosystem.

6.4.1.2 Reduction in wastewater discharge.

6.4.1.3 Creation or enhancement of Wetlands or Riparian habitats.

6.4.1.4 Reduce and Prevent Pollution.

6.4.1.5 Save Energy.

6.4.1.1 Reduce diversion of Fresh water from sensitive ecosystem

Water are generally diverted for agriculture, recreational activities, industrial and domestic purposes, which hampered sufficient water flow in natural habitat, as a result aquatic flora and fauna completely get disturbed. It also deteriorate water quality and ecosystem health. Recycled water can supplements various non-potable water demand. Thus free considerable quantity of water and increase water flow to vital ecosystem.

6.4.1.2 Reduction in wastewater discharge.

Treated wastewater are generally discharged into water body and thus sometimes changes the natural characteristic of that particular ecosystem. For instance, when high volume of treated waste water is discharged into salt water marshes, it changes it to brackish marsh. This changes also disturbs the local habitats of that ecosystem. By using recycled water and releasing less into water body protects endangered habitats also.

6.4.1.3 Creation or enhancement of Wetlands or Riparian habitats.

Wetlands are considered as a kidney of ecosystem. It is a repository of many endangered and threatened species. Recycled water can assist not only in augmenting natural wasteland and riparian habitats but also helps to create artificial wetlands. Thus helps to improve aquatic and wildlife habitats.

6.4.1.4 Reduce and Prevent Pollution.

Treated wastewater sometimes contains higher level of nutrients, such as, nitrogen, phosphorous, etc., this enhance eutrophic condition in water body thus creating eutrophication. But application of such treated water can be helpful for agriculture by decreasing the application of synthetic or chemical fertilizer. Thus recycled water can be applied for agricultural and landscape irrigation.

6.4.1.5 Save Energy

Water demand is increasing at an alarming rate. This has decrease ground water table and to extract water from ground, heavy pumps are used, which required heavy energy. For transportation of water to a distant place also needed lots of energy. Recycling water on site or nearby saves energy by decreasing the transportation of water to distant place and pumping water from deep within an aquifer. Recycled water of lower quality can used for toilet flushing. Thus save energy and it can be used only for treatment of water for drinking purposes.

6.4.2 Future of Water Recycling

Recycled water has not shown any human health hazards. It is a reliable water supply without compromising public health. It can easily cope up with the increasing water demand and can also save environment. Recycled water is a sustainable approach and cost effective as it saves lots of energy and fresh water. World is already facing shortage of water and by year 2040, thirty three countries will face extremely high water stress condition. This is inevitable to save water resources by diverting treated wastewater for non-potable use of water.

6.5 Water Management for Agriculture

Water is critically essential for agriculture as even good seeds and proper fertilizer could not come up with a good yield unless until plant is optimally watered. The world's population is expected to grow up to 10 billion by 2050. India, at present, accounts for approximately 17 percent of the world's population and it is likely to increase to 1.6 billion by 2050, resulting intensification of demand for more energy, food and water. The demand is increasing at alarming rates but at the same time the supply is decreasing at staggering rate.

According to Food and Agriculture Organization of the United Nation, more than third of the world's irrigated area is functioned by groundwater. In India, agriculture accounts for 90 percent of ground water and overutilization on irrigated agriculture resulted in falling of ground water table at the rate of 2 to 3 meter per year. It was reported by Asian Water Development Outlook Report (2016) that agriculture alone consumes 80 percent of water in Asia and Pacific region. The most challenging task before decision makers, researchers, scientists is to double food production as well as water sources by year 2050 to meet the requirements of growing population. At the same time impacts of climate change and climate variability all over the world also intensify these challenges.

In agriculture, irrigation system mainly harvest large quantities of water and generally water is used carelessly eventually leading to wastage of water. It is reported that 70 percent of the fresh water is consumed by agriculture. Agriculture is both a user as well as a producer of waste water. The global water demand of agriculture by year 2050 is expected to rise by 19 percent due to irrigational needs. In South East Asian region, which is densely populated, food is mostly cultivated in artificially irrigated areas and reported 40 percent of the world food is grown in artificially irrigated areas. In India, agricultural sector uses alone approximately 92 percent of groundwater and 89 percent of surface water.

It is reported by Food and Agriculture Organization's AQUASTAT that out of total water withdrawal worldwide, which is approximately 3,928 km³ per year, agriculture drainage and wastewater alone accounts for 1,257 km³ per year, which is 32 percent of the total. Therefore, agriculture where maximum amount of fresh water is used and as the world is facing challenge of water stress, it is inevitable to shift to alternative sources to meet out the agricultural requirement. Moreover efficient application of water in agriculture also reduces water demand to some extent. There are several ways to reduce the consumption of water or can efficiently use water for agriculture such as, drip irrigation, dry farming, irrigation scheduling, shifting to organic, conservation tillage, drought-tolerant crops, compost and mulching, etc.

6.5.1 Irrigation System

In India, the methodology of irrigation mainly involves flood irrigation, which consumes lots of water and carelessly uses also result in excessive loss of water. This practice can be reduce by using efficient ways of irrigation, such as, drip (trickle) irrigation or sprinkler irrigation. The drip or trickle irrigation method is also refer as Micro-irrigation system (MIS). These methods are applicable for all sort of crops.

In *Sprinkler Irrigation*, water is applied only once in four to seven days. This decreases the moisture stress of the crop area and water can be applied whenever it is needed. This method has an efficiency of 70 to 75 percent. However, this involves more energy and more labour. It cannot be considered as better alternative.

In *Drip (trickle) Irrigation,* water is directly applied to a plant's root, thus decreasing the evaporation that generally occurs with spray watering system. There is no water or moisture stress. This method reduces water loss and if properly implemented, this can conserve water up to 80 percent and can even contribute to increased crop yields. Water is applied in controlled manner and only requisite quantity of water is given to each plant based on the evapotranspiration requirements. This method has an efficiency of 90 to 95 percent and considered as better alternative for irrigation. This method is also known as Micro-Irrigation system (MIS) and has following prominent characteristics-

- Water application is at a low rate,
- After a long period of time, water is applied,
- Water uses at frequent intervals,
- It delivers water directly to plants root zone,
- Application of water is done through a low pressure delivery system,
- It saves water up to 80 percent.
- It is cost-effective and easy in operation,
- There is no soil erosion and crop productivity is also increases,

- It requires less labour and less energy,
- Fertilizers can also be injected directly through this system,
- It is suitable for any sort of crops as well as soil,
- It is applicable and efficiently workout even in poor soil,
- Salt water can also be used under drip irrigation to some extent,
- Annual electricity charges are less and water can applied without any loss,
- Land levelling is not required as all types of undulating lands can be irrigated,
- Wind has no impact on drip irrigation, even under heavy windy conditions water can be effectively applied.

6.5.2 Capturing and Storing of Water

Water can be stored in artificial ponds or tanks during rainy season or excess of water, which can be used for multiple activities. It is better to develop micro-water structure for rainwater or surface runoff water harvesting. This increases the water productivity and also ensures water throughout the year. By creating artificial storage system for water, like pond, not only support agriculture but also helps in fish or poultry farms. This enhances the livelihood strategies and ensures sustainability of ecosystem.

6.5.3 Irrigation Scheduling

Smart water management means not only to use water efficiently but also to apply it only when needed. It is essential to know when, how much, and how often water is needed by each plants. Farmers need to carefully monitor the weather forecast and also time to time monitor soil and water moisture to avert under or over watering of their crops. In this method by keeping check on weather forecast, rainfall can be applied as much as possible. This requires effective and proper scheduling of irrigation timing. This is basically a practical tool for averting over application of water and maintaining crop growth simultaneously. This methodologies also diminishes the burden on natural water resources as well as on energy. By maintaining the timing of irrigation, it reduces excessive use of pumps to withdraw water continuously.

There are three methodologies which can be applied to measure the crop water use, that is,

- Evapotranspiration measurement,
- Soil water measurement, and
- Plant water measurement.

6.5.4 Rotational Grazing

Rotational grazing is one of the methodology where livestock are deliberately moved between fields. This movement of livestock assist in promoting pasture regrowth. It also enhances the field's water absorption, making pasture more drought resistant, increases soil organic matter, better forage cover as well as reduces surface water runoff. This is dual benefits for farmers which keep their fields as well as animals healthy.

6.5.5 Dry Farming

Dry farming is one of the methodologies which is based on microclimates and depends completely on soil moisture to produce their crops during dry season. This yields less in comparison to irrigated crops. Such farming is more common in California where it is used for raising potato, apple, grapes, olives, etc.

6.5.6 Conservation Tillage

Conservation tillage is the methodologies which involves partially tillage and leave 30 percent of crops residue on the surface. This practice decreases evaporation, soil erosion as well as compaction and augmented water absorption capacity of the land. There are several ways by which conservation tillage can be applied, such as, No-Till, Ridge-Till, Strip-Till, Mulch-Till, and Reduced-Till.

6.5.7 Compost, Mulch, and Organic Farming

The compost, mulch when applied as a fertilizer or shifted to organic farming helps to improve the soil structure and enhances the water holding capacity. Mulch is basically a material, such as, wood chips, or straw etc. which is usually spread on top of the surface soil to converse moisture. It is made up of organic material which will gradually breakdown into compost by microbial action, thereby increasing the fertility of soil as well as retain moisture content. Soil gradually becomes rich in organic matter and serves as a sponge which provides moisture to plants.

6.5.8 Water User Association (WUA)

Water management can be successfully achieve only when it involves all the stakeholder. Farmers are the major stakeholder of water, thus it is essential to involve them at local level to effectively manage water. Water User Association (WUA) is basically a cooperative association of individual water users who wish to undertake water related activities for their mutual benefits. This association is need to develop and strengthened at each local level. It is based on the concept on 'Participatory Irrigation Management.' It is reported by Global Forum for Food and Agriculture (2017) that in India approximately 56,539 WUA manages 13.16 million hectare of irrigated land. The function of water user association involves,

- Proper water distribution to each farmers (Rich, poor, or marginal farmers).
- Provision of drinking water from canals.
- WUA acts as an interface between the farmers and the main system management.
- Proper and effective drainage.
- WUA has a managing committee which attends all day today functioning.

WUA in India started in 1987 with the advocacy of National Water Policy, based on participation of users. Further, in 1987, Ministry of Water Resources, Government of India issued guidelines for the formation of Water User Association. This ensures water distribution among all stakeholders. It motivate farmers for group actions, especially for channel maintenance. This maintain channels in good condition, also maintain and monitor the condition of structure, channels and also resolves any conflicts among farmers and protect crops against damage by cattle. The WUA has committee which discuss and decide potential crops, coordinate channels, and planned canal operation. This has helps to reduce water losses, increases crop yield and area irrigated per unit volume of water has increased by 15.12 percent. It has also brought down various environmental problems, such as, soil salinity, soil erosion, water logging, etc.

6.5.9 General Methodologies for Management of Water in Agriculture

There are several methods which can be applied to conserve water. Such as,

- Farming technique of better quality should be adopted to minimize the demand of water to the field.
- The canal must be competently lined on its sides and bottom to minimize the seepage. It would be better if it is covered to reduce the evaporation.
- Integrated Intensive Farming System (IIFS) or Ecological Farming System (EFS) involves agricultural intensification, diversification and value addition. It involves the extensive use of farm resources, for instance, irrigated rice along with fish, vegetable, fruits, poultry, and other crops in mixed or rotational practices with appropriate combination.
- Develop strategies of integrated watershed development for efficient rainwater use and management.
- Conveyance of water through pipes to prevent seepage and transportation losses.
- Providing drainage facilities in the canal and tank commercial area to increase productivity and applying the drainage water for irrigation.
- Integrated watershed development should be undertaken to apply rain water, ground water, surface runoff, and soil water to increase the production in rainfed areas.
- Construction of check dams or small dams and percolation ponds to conserve water.
- Application of salt or brackish water by selecting suitable crops depending on the quality of water.
- Involvement of farmers and Non-governmental organization (NGO) to create awareness about water stress or scarcity and to take up better water management practices.
- Strengthening Water User Association (WUA) at local level.
- More attention to research in water technology to harvest, conserve, and application of water in optimum manner.
- Assessment of water pollution vulnerabilities and development strategies for their control.

6.6 Water Management at Household

Water is mostly waste due to the negligence usually shown by all of us. The little efforts from each and every one side could solve the problem of water scarcity. The sensible and efficient use of water can avert many water crisis situation. There are several ways to conserve water at domestic level, such as,

- All taps and pipes should be clearly checked to avoid any sort of water leakage.
- The continued flow of water can be avoided during shaving, teeth brushing, cloth or floor washing etc. It can be used when needed.
- Vehicles can be wipe using wet cloth or sponge instead of using pipe water or hose to reduce water quantity. Use spray nozzle when rinsing for efficient use. Waterless car washing system can also be used. Recycled water or rain water can be used for the same purpose. This simple practice can save up to 150 gallons of water.
- Toilet flushing should have two switches for minimum and maximum use of water, which can be used accordingly. It is better to install saving showerheads and ultra-low-flush toilet.
- To irrigate kitchen garden or lawn, drip irrigation or direct sprinkling of water can be used.
- Most important rainwater harvesting system should be installed to avoid wastage of water.
- If rainwater harvesting system is not possible due to any reason, rainwater can be harvest using simple bucket or diverting drain pipes directly to kitchen gardens or lawn.
- Stop using toilet as a wastebasket. As every time flushing even small bit of trash consume five to seven gallon of water.
- Always use full loads in washing machine and dishwasher. This will avert wastage of water.
- Always purchase water saving products. Plenty of it are available in market whether it is water saving taps, showerheads, or washing machine etc.
- Installing a water meter is also a better way to check utility and wastage of water. Either pay for use or check uses, in both cases water meter assist to save water.

A passing thought before closing this section is – what are those small steps which can be done to save water at our own? There are various small steps which can be taken to conserve water, such as, turn off the tap while brushing, this would save 6 litre of water per minute. Place a cistern displacement device in the toilet cistern to reduce the volume of water during each flush. Always use full loads of washings machine and dish washer. Fix a dripping tap, this could save 15 litre of water a day. Install a water butt to drain pipes and use the water collected to water plants, clean car and for washing windows, floor, etc.

CHAPTER VII

Policy Dimension

"Act together – Water is everybody's Business"

– Anonymous

7.1 Introduction

Expert believes that water scarcity is not really a man-made or natural disaster, but actually a 'government – made disaster.' India is well-blessed nation in the world in terms of average rainfall, approximately precipitation is 105 cm per year, and there is no reason why India should suffer from water scarcity. Though various rules, regulations, and programme are meant by government at rural and urban level to conserve water, but often on papers and poorly implemented on reality or on ground. Therefore, the foremost step or the bigger challenge is to bring all those rules, regulation and programme in reality on ground. However, the picture is also not very disheartening as the situation has awakened not only India but whole world to seriously focus on the way to protect natural resources or environment in totality for the survival of human being. India has shown its sincerity and also understand the need to protect resources or mother earth since 1972 that can be shown by the statement given by Mrs. Indira Gandhi, the late Prime minister of India at UN Conference on Environment at Stockholm (Sweden) on June 14, 1972:

'Modern man must re-establish his unbroken link with nature and with life. He must again learn to invoke the energy and to recognize, as did the ancients in India centuries ago, that we can take from the earth and atmosphere only so much as one put back into them.'

Besides the 2016 UN World Water Development Report, *'Water and Jobs'* projected that three out of four jobs that constitute the entire global workforce are water dependent and that more than 1.4 billion jobs or say 42 percent of the World's active workforce, are profoundly dependent on water. Water is considered as a key factor for human survival. It also plays a vital role in the development of job opportunities. There is a direct opportunity of management of water resources or those economic sectors that are heavily dependent on water resources, such as, agriculture, fishing, power industries, and health sectors. Besides educated and healthy workforce is possible only with a good and safe supply of drinking water and sanitation.

The report on 'Asian Water Future and Solution 2050' prepared by the International Institute for Applied Systems Analysis estimated that up to 3.4 billion people could be living in water stressed area of Asia by 2050. Climate change is exaggerating water scarcity problem. The coming next few decades will be an eyewitness of multiple challenges at the connection of water, food as well as energy. In 2016 it was considered that the most influential risk over the next 10 years will be the water crisis or water scarcity, strengthening 'water security' as an urgent political matter. It is now become an essentiality to increase political backing and action for sustainable water resources development.

Before addressing the issue of water scarcity, it is essential to know that water scarcity can be resulted from two mechanism of –

–   Physical water scarcity, and
–   Economic water scarcity.

Physical (Absolute) water scarcity

This has resulted from insufficient natural water resources to meet the demand and it is estimated that around one fifth of the world's population resides in a region of physical or absolute water scarcity. Arid regions are mostly affected with physical scarcity of water. This scarcity also occurs when demand exceeds supply of water or water resources are over committed, such as, hydraulic infrastructure constructed for irrigation. The symptoms includes environmental degradation as well as declining groundwater and over exploitation of resources.

Economic water scarcity

This is caused due to lack of investment in technology or infrastructure to withdraw water from any water resources, be it a river or aquifer. This is a result of human failure to meet the demand for water. It is estimated that approximately one quarter of the world's population is suffering from economic scarcity of water. As a consequence people need to travel a long distance to fetch water and that also highly contaminated water for either their daily uses or for irrigation purpose. Africa is a better example of economic scarcity of water which can be resolved by constructing water infrastructure in those areas. Communities residing in arid regions suffered critically due to weak economy as well as poor policies. Such countries where water scarcity is a major issue needs to revise their policies.

The United Nation Committee on Economic, Social, and Cultural Rights declares 'Right to Water' for every human, which entitles everyone to harmless, adequate, satisfactory, easily available and inexpensive water for daily uses as well as for other uses.

7.2 Millennium Development Goals and Water Resources

During Millennium Summit in 2000, the United Nation addressed the issue of economic water scarcity and thus ensures access to safe drinking water to everyone as an international development goals. Millennium Development Goal (MDG) drafted during this summit has in total eight goals. The Seventh Goal of MDG sets a target for decreasing the proportion of the population deprived of sustainable drinking water access by half by 2015. This seventh goal ensures that more than 600 million people would gain entrance to a safe drinking water. The MDG 7 also acts as an indicator to quantify the level of human pressure on water resources, based on the relation between supply and demand for water. Millennium Development Goal seven has four targets. These are as follows:

1. To assimilate the principles of sustainable development into every nation's policies and programme and also reverse the depletion of environmental resources.
2. To decrease biodiversity loss and accomplish a substantial reduction in the rate of loss by 2010.
3. To halve the proportion of the universal population without sustainable access to clean and safe drinking water and basic sanitation by 2015.
4. To accomplish substantial improvement in the lives of a minimum of 100 million slum dwellers by 2020.

Goal 7 of MDG has accomplish some of the achievements which are as follows;

1. Since 1990, it is estimated that there is a substantial increase in marine and terrestrial protected areas. It is recorded that in Caribbean and Latin America, the coverage of terrestrial protected areas has increased from 8.8 percent in 1990 to 23.4 percent in 2014.
2. The percentage of people having access to drinking water sources has increased from 76 percent in 1990 to 91 percent in 2015.
3. Since 1990, approximately 2.6 billion people has gained access to safe drinking water. Of these approximately 1.9 billion people has gained access to piped drinking water on premises, with 58 percent of the global population gained this level of service in 2015.

4. Almost 147 nations has achieved the drinking water target fulfilling goal 7 of MDG. Out of which 95 nations has achieved the sanitation target and 77 nations has achieved both drinking water as well as sanitation target.

5. Since 1990, the proportion of open defecation has reduced by nearly 50 percent and approximately 2.1 billion people has gained improved sanitation all over the world.

6. From 2000 to 2014, it was noticed that the proportion of urban population in developing nation residing in slums has decreased from 39.4 to 29.7 percent.

Based on four targets of Goal 7 of MDG, progress or regress are as follows;

Target 1 to 4:

It is estimated that the net loss in forest cover has reduced from 8.3 million hectare annually in 1990 to 5.2 million hectare annually each year between 2000 and 2010. The net loss of forest or the rate of deforestation has slightly reduced and there is an increase in afforestation as well as the natural expansion of forest cover in some part of the world. Asia region has shown net gain of 2.2 million hectare of forest cover annually from 2000 to 2010. However South America, Oceania, and Africa has shown significant net losses of forest cover due to severe drought and forest fires in Oceania.

Secondly, there is no improvement in global greenhouse gases reduction. The greenhouse gases, especially, carbon dioxide has significantly increased by over 50 percent from 1990 to 2012. This increment in greenhouse gas emission has further warm the planet, eventually leading to long lasting changes in the climate system, thus exaggerating the problems of food shortages and water scarcity as well as longer lasting weather extremes.

Thirdly, it is estimated that from 1974 to 2011, there is a significant reduction of marine fish stock within safe biological limits has dropped by 19 percent, that is, from 90 percent to 71 percent. As a consequences, fish stock are found to be below the level at which they can maximize sustainable yields in 2015. However, in certain areas of Europe, North America, and Oceania have effectively rebuilt some of their over fished stocks.

Fourth, in spite of some improvement which has indicated as achievement of Goal 7 of MDG, water scarcity has significantly increased. It is estimated that water stress areas has increased in 41 countries in 2011, which is higher than 1998, when it was only 36 countries experiencing water stress. The worst situation is from the Arabian Peninsula, Northern Africa, and Central Asia, where withdrew of water is more than 100 percent, this means that they are depleting their renewable groundwater resources at fast rate.

Finally we can say, some targets have been achieved but for some it is still need to work. The environmental sustainability or sustainable development is still a core pillar of the post – 2015 agenda. The MDG has ended in 2015, and in 2016 the Millennium Development Goal (MDG) is replaced with the Sustainable Development Goals (SDG).

7.3 Sustainable Development Goal (SDG) and Water Resources

The Sustainable Development Goals replaces Millennium Development Goal, has in total 17 goals and 169 targets. This covers a wide range of social, economic and development issues. The SDG is also refer as '*Transforming our World: the 2030 Agenda for Sustainable Development*' or *2030 Agenda* in short. The MDG framework has distinguished between developed and developing nation but SDG framework does not differentiate rather equally apply to all nations. This resolution which involved 193 member states, is a broad intergovernmental agreement which acts as the Post-2015 Development Agenda.

Goal 6 of SDG ensures clean water and sanitation. The theme of goal 6 states that 'Ensure availability and sustainable management of water and sanitation for all.' The SDG goal 6 has in total eight targets and 11 indicators that will be applied to monitor progress towards the targets. The deadline given to achieve these all are by the year 2030 and one is targeted for 2020.

The first three targets are associated with drinking water supply and sanitation. It is reported that clean and safe drinking water as well as hygienic toilets protect people from various diseases and thus make societies to be economically more productive. A healthy body gives a healthy mind. The 'Equitable sanitation' is called for and calls for addressing the specific needs of women and girls, elderly or people with disabilities. Water resources can be better protected and preserved if open defecation is ended as well as sustainable sanitation systems are implemented. The main indicator of the sanitation targets is the '*Proportion of population using safely managed sanitation services, including a hand washing facilities with soap and water.*' The Sustainable Sanitation Alliance (SuSanA) has created its mission to accomplish SDG goal 6. Since SDG are highly interdependent, therefore, the provision of clean water and sanitation for all is basically a forerunner to achieving many of the other SDGs. Box 7.1 indicates the water goals and its target.

Box 7.1 Water Goals and its targets

The Water Goals and its Targets

SDG Goal 6: Ensure availability and sustainability management of water and sanitation for all.

Targets under Goal 6 to achieve by 2030:

Target 1:Universal and equitable access to safe and affordable drinking water for all.

Target 2: Access to adequate and equitable sanitation and hygiene for all, and end open defecation, paying special attention to the needs of women and girls and those in   vulnerable situations.

Target 3: Improve water quality by reducing pollution, eliminating dumping and minimizing release of hazardous chemicals and materials, halving the proportions of untreated wastewater, and at least doubling recycling and safe re-use globally.

Target 4: Increased water use efficiency across all sectors and ensures sustainable withdrawals and supply of freshwater to address water scarcity, and substantially reduce the number of people suffering from water scarcity.

Target 5: Implement IWRM (Integrated water resource management) at all levels, including through transboundary cooperation as appropriate.

Target 6: By 2020, protect and restore water related ecosystem, including forest, wetlands, river, mountain, aquifer, and lakes.

(Source: UN Department of Economic and Social Affairs, Division for Sustainable Development. 2015. Sustainable Development Know Platform. Accessed 15th Jan. 2018 from http://sustainabledevelopment. un.org/sdg6.)

Integrated Water Resource Management (IWRM) was initially adopted for the first time at the World Summit on Sustainable Development, Johannesburg in 2002, which was later reaffirmed in 2012 at the UN conference on Sustainable Development, Rio + 20. The IWRM is finally incorporated as Target 5 of Goal 6 of SDGs.

The SDG goals were highly criticized. Some of the criticism cited below;

1. It was said that SDG is highly contradictory. Three sectors, that is, environment, equity or social, and economy, need to come together and requires the promotion of transdisciplinary and multidisciplinary research across different sectors, in order to accomplish SDG. However it is difficult to bring them together in an effective way.

2. 'The Economist' in 2015 debated that 169 targets for the SDGs is too lengthy, communicating them as 'sprawling, misconceived, and a mess' compared to MDGs. It was further argued that the goal has ignored local context and all other 16 goals might be conditional on achieving SDG goal 1. However, almost all stakeholders engaged in negotiation to develop SDGs seems to be in accord that the high number of 17 goals justified as the agenda they address is all incorporating.

3. According to 'The Economist' the high cost seems to be a hurdle in achieving SDGs. It is estimated that alleviating poverty and accomplishing the other sustainable SDGs will require almost about 2–3 trillion USD per year for the next 15 years, which is highly ambitious and 'pure fantasy.' The estimation to provide clean drinking water and sanitation for the whole population of all continents is approximately as high as 200 billion USD. However, the World Bank warned that estimates required to be made country by country, instead of as whole and reevaluated frequently over time.

The Sustainable development goal is an outcome of a UN conference that was highly appreciated by non-governmental organization (NGOs). It receives huge support from this sector. In comparison with MDGs, SDGs deals more with the causes of the problems and it is all about sustainable development, whereas MDG was highly criticized by NGOs as it was not only dealing with the problems but only focused on development not sustainable development. Moreover MDG used a storage tower approach to problems whereas the SDGs taken into consideration the inter-connectedness of all the problems.

When we say '*Water Security*,' this is elaborated by UN University 2013, A UN-Water Analytical Brief. Ontario: UN Institute for water, Environment and Health, states –"*The capacity of a population to safeguard sustainable access to adequate quantities of acceptable quality water for sustaining livelihoods, human well-being and socio-economic development, for ensuring protection against water borne pollution and water related disasters and for preserving ecosystems in a climate of peace and political stability.*"

The water security can only be achieved by the societies only when the water resources and services are successfully managed –

- to satisfy household water as well as sanitation requirement in all communities,
- to support productive economies in industries, energy and agricultural sectors,
- to improve energetic, convenient, vibrant cities and towns,
- to reestablish healthy, vigorous rivers and ecosystem, and
- to build strong communities that can able to adapt to change (Source: Asia Water Development Outlook Report (AWDO), 2016).

Further, Asia Water Development Outlook, 2016 reported to enumerate complete water security, water security framework was developed along with five interdependent key dimensions, which are described as follows:

- Household water security,
- Economic water security,
- Urban water security,
- Environmental water security, and
- Resilience to water related diseases.

Asia Water Development Outlook describes five stages or five index to assess the National Water Security. The overall national water security is given a score from 1 to 100 and is the sum of the key dimension scores.

At National water security Index 1 involves those situation which is considered to be hazardous and the gap is enormous between the current status and the acceptable or standard levels of water security.

At National water security Index 5 involves those situation which can be set up as model country for performing exemplary in management of water resources and services and the country is completely water secure as realistically possible. The stages or index chosen by Asia Water Development Outlook 2016 was the same as in taken in 2013.

At National water security Index 2 involves those countries where more than halve of the population have access to modest drinking water and sanitation facilities and water services are at the starting stage. This also indicate that those countries have taken measures to improve their water quality and in priority are addressing water related risks. Table 7.1 indicates the index and the score given accordingly (Source: AWDO, 2016)

Table 7.1 National Water Security Index and Scores (*Sources: AWDO, 2016*)

Index	Score	Stages
5	96 and above	Model
4	76 < 96	Effective
3	56 < 76	Capable
2	36 < 56	Engaged
1	0 < 36	Hazardous

At the National water security Index 3 involves those countries which have access to safe and clean drinking water as well as sanitation facilities and it is reaching to even rural and poor areas. Water quality is at the stage of improving and measures have already taken to rejuvenate ecological health of the water resources as well as the most dangerous water related hazards are also being addressed.

At the National water security Index 4 involves those countries where almost all people have access to safe drinking water and sanitation facilities. The quality of water is in the acceptable level and water service are also appropriate to support economic development. Further attention is now towards restoration of ecological health by improving water resources and water related hazards are seriously brought to less by applying all warning system as well as infrastructure.

It is reported through Joint Monitoring Programme (JMP) issued by WHO and UNICEF that the Asia and Pacific region has shown progress in accomplishing 2015 Millennium Development Goal (MDG) on drinking water as well as sanitation facilities with an exception of Oceania, Caucasus or Central Asia region. This report also focused on the inequalities or gap left between poor and rich, both in rural and urban area.

The Water for All Policy 2001 was adopted to establish a link between water related challenges as well as poverty reduction and regional development associated with it. It is essential to appropriately manage water resources and services both effectively and efficiently. Further the water operational plan (2011–2020) established basic fundamental principle within the operational context.

7.4 Water Scarcity - A Challenge

The population of South Asia is projected to grow by 32 percent in three decades – from 1.68 billion in 2010 to about 2.22 billion in 2040. The consequences will be higher competition over water among industries, urban centers, rural, agriculture sectors as well as among South Asian countries, those who shares common transboundary rivers or water resources. The reason for this speedy decline in physical water availability is mainly arises due to-

- Expanding economic activity,
- Rapid urbanization, and
- Changing consumption patterns.

The Indicator which is generally used to indicate water stress is Falkenmark Water Stress Indicator. This gives one metric for gauging the adequacy of water supplies and this considers 1700 m³ per person per year to be the national threshold for achieving water requirement for agriculture, domestic and industrial use. As per Falkenmark Water Stress Indicator water level below 1000 m³ indicates 'water scarcity' zone whereas the water level below 500 m³ represents the area of 'absolute scarcity.' It is reported that in several areas in India and Pakistan, groundwater level is falling at the speed of one to three meter per year. The physical scarcity of water is usually compounded by economic scarcity. This eventually results an unsustainable situation where it is difficult to meet current needs as well as generate the resources for creating future infrastructure. Further the World Bank has warned India that it might be possible that there will be shortage of water supplies by

2050. Bangladesh, Bhutan and India have formulated their National Water Policies to address water related issues.

Transboundary River are extremely prone to pollution by the fact that there are over two hundred rivers or other water resources in the world that shares two or more than two countries. The 'Helsinki Rule' was also adopted on the uses of water of transboundary or international rivers. This is an important guideline regulating river and their connected groundwater that cross national boundaries. It was adopted by the International Law Association (ILA) in Helsinki, Finland (August 1966).

Australia

It has variable rainfall and climate yet it is the driest inhabited continent in terms of average precipitation. Climate Change has aggravated the problem of water scarcity. The Southeastern Murray-Darling Basin is threatened with severe water stress, on this more than two third of population of Australia depends for their water uses. The Australian government in 2008 had invested approximately 9 billion USD for modernization and improvement of their irrigation system and restoration of ecological health. The Government of Australia played a vital role in resolving many of their issues related to water stress.

Bangladesh

It has the third largest population suffering from poverty and water related disaster. As per the report given by United Nation Development Programme states that four out of five people in Bangladesh live below the poverty line and one out of three lives in extreme poverty. The poor people are more vulnerable to water borne diseases due to unsafe drinking water and sanitation facilities. The three major rivers flows through Bangladesh yet water stress is major challenge. Climate Change is adding the problem to extreme disrupting livelihood and the economy. Bangladesh government has major challenges but can resolve their issues through proper coordination among different sectors of the communities.

China

The world's highest population, expected to grow to 1.42 billion by 2050. Urbanization and development is drastically threatening the water resources. Desertification and Climate Change is estimated to exaggerate the water scarcity. Despite of having three major rivers basins – the Huai, Hai and Huang (Yellow) rivers yet facing scarcity of water. It is projected that Climate Change will reduce China's glacial coverage by 27 percent by 2050. Besides food insecurity problems are also raising and social as well as political tension that are attributable to water pollution have already emerged in China.

Indonesia

It has become pollution hub due to its rapid urbanization, industrialization and economic development. In Indonesia, more than 70 percent of population depends on potentially contaminated sources. Climate Change is exaggerating the challenges by disrupting the regular, arid dryness as well as alternating periods of rain. Therefore, managing water scarcity is a critical challenge for Indonesia and for many South Asian countries with similar condition.

Malaysia

It has huge freshwater resources. It is not considered as water stressed nation in general. But rapid industrialization and urbanization are increasing pollution levels become a reason of concern. Climate Change is also threatening Malaysia to a large extent.

Pakistan

It is considered as one of the most water stressed nations. High demand of water from agriculture sector, industries and domestic sector has lead to severe water stressed condition. Its population is also growing at faster rate. The migration to urban areas and decreasing economic practices in rural areas has worsened the situation, increasing enormous challenges.

India

India's population is expected to grow to 1.4 billion by 2025. Urbanization and Industrialization has demanded water at huge level as well as high demand from agriculture has compounded the problem of water scarcity. Climate Change is also intensifying the cycle and magnifies the consequences. India has adopted National Water Policy, which was formulated by Ministry of Water Resources, Government of India, in 1987 and this reviewed and updated in 2002 and then in 2012. To fetch huge population and meet out water requirement, the one concept given was National River Linking project. This project is highly ambitious related to inter-basin water transfer project but it was criticized by suggesting that tampering with nature on such a huge scale would sooner or later brings a ecological disaster.

India has water storage capacity of approximately 253 billion cubic meters (BCM). The major provisions under the national water policy are;

— Visualize establishing a standard national information system with a network of databank and data basis.
— Resources planning and recycling for providing maximum availability.
— Importance is given to the impact of projects on human settlements and environment.
— Guidelines for the safety of storage dams and other water related structure.
— Regulating exploitation of groundwater resources.

- Settling water allocation priorities in following order: Drinking water, Irrigation, Hydropower, Navigation, Industries and other uses.
- The water rates for groundwater as well as surface water should be rationalized with due regards to the interest of small and marginal farmers.
- This policy also focused and emphasis the participation of famers and voluntary agencies to protect water quality, flood and drought management, erosions, etc.

The main emphasis of National Water Policy of 2012 is to consider water as 'economic good.' But this was criticized and finally adopted with disapproval from many states in India. This policy does not follow 'Polluter pays Principle' rather it provides incentives for effluents treatments.

The draft of National Water Policy of 2016 comes with the principle for protection, conservation, as well as regulation and management of water as vital and stressed natural resources. In India 'Water' comes in the state list of the constitution. Therefore, states of India also play a vital role in implementation of these rules and regulation considering water as 'Right to water life.'

7.5 Author Point of View

Most of the politicians are unaware with the importance or requirement of water management. Environmental issues most of the time takes a back seat in election time, as far as India is concerned. Moreover the fact is that the communities and individuals hardly aware with their own rights to ask politicians about 'safe water, safe air, and safe land.' Policy makers seems to be little indifferent or very poorly responsive to the ecological as well as socio-economic and cultural circumstances of different regions, exaggerating the menace of water scarcity. Besides water users and communities themselves plays a little role in the overall conservation and management of water resources. Quality of water is also a paramount aspect of water policy as poor water quality is responsible for various water borne diseases. The one way which was adopted worldwide to evade water pollution or any sort of pollution is the introduction of the 'Polluter pays Principle.' But this principle, in other way, also suggest that one who has enough money has all rights to pollute and get away by giving lump sum amount or fine. This also reflects the overconfidence of policy makers or decision makers on various pollution mitigating technologies, as well as, such policies takes very easily environment overall at backseat, giving an easy going attitude towards environment. The result of which is in one shape of 'water scarcity.' Expert's views says that very soon in near future just like gold or oil, water will also become a commodity and wars will be fought over who possesses the water supply. In 2008, Ban Ki Moon UN Secretary General warned 'A shortage of water resources could spell increase conflicts in the future.'

The 'Polluter pays Principle' can be applicable where it is needed to mitigate pollution but it can be a threat as one way it also gives freedom to pollute with a condition to pay. Such policies are strongly needed to modify as environment or any natural resources once polluted or contaminated is hard to rejuvenate and it is also a time taking process. We should not forget that whatever achievements we made ultimately we all are living on this earth and have no other alternative. Even economic growth would be at one point get halt if there is no natural resources exist as a raw material. Since 1972, when world attended first UN conference on human environment at Stockholm, almost all nations pledged to protect all natural resources and utilized them efficiently and effectively, but living in 2018 seems we can easily forgets all pledge or too busy to protect environment. Already completed 23 Conference of parties (COP) and at every meeting it is pledged to protect and conserve natural resources, but the achievement is little different from what we pledged. Till-to-date roughly 2.4 billion people are still living in water stressed countries and projected that by 2025 the number would rise to two third. By 2050 it is projected that freshwater availability in South-East, Central, East, and South Asia, is estimated to drastically reduce leading more than 40 percent of the world's population in water stress or chronic water scarcity. Perhaps we are in habit of taking natural resources for granted. The most essential element of life is most simple things, needed for survival, but are mostly neglected.

At this level I would like to suggest to policy makers or decision makers that instead of taking 'Polluter pays Principle,' it is better to adopt new 'Polluter works Principle' or 'Polluter responsibility Principle.' When we say 'Polluter works Principle' or 'Polluter responsibility Principle,' it means whoever pollute must take complete accountability and responsibility to mitigate pollution and ensure the rejuvenation of that natural resources. For instance, if an industry dump their waste water without any treatment into river body, the responsible company has to take all accountability and responsibility to rejuvenate that river body or water resources to its natural condition with all water quality, and till then company would lose permit to work in that zone. The Pollution Control Board would work as a monitoring agency to ensure that company is taking responsibility. The same principle can be applied at an individual level. We should not forget that the major challenge world is facing today is how to balance supply and demand of natural resources. Therefore, it become more important to conserve whatever the natural resources we have, improving artificial resources as well as rejuvenating the existing resources to meet the demand of huge population. This become increasingly relevant as we are marching towards a phase of uncertainty which is linked to climate change and variability.

Besides hunger and poverty are also one of the reason that leads to over exploitation of natural resources. Protecting environment is not a specific area, it has various areas interlinked with it which is directly or indirectly related to human survival. Without food security and standard economic living, it is hard to believe to achieve all the goals set up in Sustainable Development Goal (SDG). The healthy, diverse and well managed ecosystem is interlinked with economic growth, and this also plays a vital role in improving the livelihoods and mitigating future challenges. This could only be achieved by proper cooperation and behavior change among politicians, governments, civil society, as well as communities as a whole.

7.6 Conferences on Water Security

The upcoming conferences on drinking water and sanitation facilities are as follows;

1. The Water Show Africa 2018, Johannesburg, South Africa, 27th–28th March 2018.
2. Seventh South Asia Conference on Sanitation, (SACOSAN 7), Islamabad, Pakistan, 10th–13th April 2018.
3. The Global Water Summit-12th year, Paris, France on 15th–17th April 2018.
4. Launch of United Nation – Water SDG 6 – 2018 Synthesis Report on Water and Sanitation in the 2030 Agenda – May 2018.
5. SWAN (Smart Water: Meeting Tomorrow's Challenges Today), Barcelona, Spain, 21st–22nd May 2018.
6. Sludge Management in Circular Economy, Rome, Italy, 23rd–25th May, 2018.
7. Fifth Water India Expo, New Delhi, India, 23rd–25th May 2018.
8. The International high level conference on International decade for Action, "Water for Sustainable Development, 2018–2028 to be held from 20th to 22nd June 2018 in Dushanbe, Tajikistan.
9. First International Conference on 'Water Security' on 17th–20th June 2018, Toronto, Canada.
10. Rotary International Convention, Toronto, Canada, 24th–27th June, 2018.
11. Thirty Fourth AGUASAN Workshop, "Leveraging the data revolution-informed decision making for better water and sanitation management," Spiez, Switzerland, 25th–29th June, 2018.
12. Singapore International Water Week (SIWW), 8th–12th July 2018, Singapore.
13. Forty First WEDC International Conference Transformations towards Sustainable and Resilient WASH Services, Nakuru, Kenya, 9th–13th July 2018.
14. High level Political Forum 2018: Transformation towards sustainable and resilient societies (SDG 6, 7, 11, 12, 15) on 9th–18th July 2018, New York, USA
15. DT 2018 – Sixth International Dry Toilet Conference, on 22nd–24th August 2018, Tampere, Finland.
16. World Water Week 2018: Water, Ecosystem and Human Development, on 26th–31st August 2018, Stockholm, Sweden.
17. Global Water Security Conference for Agriculture and natural Resources, 3rd–6th October 2018, Hyderabad, India.

18. Fifteen IWA Specialized Conference on small water and wastewater system and seventh specialized conference on resources oriented sanitation, on 14th–18th October 2018, Haifa, Israel.
19. IFAT India: Trade Fair for water, sewage, solid waste and recycling, on 15th–17th October 2018, Mumbai, Maharashtra, India
20. Eighth International Conferences and Exhibition on water, wastewater and environmental monitoring (WWEM 2018), on 21st–22nd November 2018, England, United Kingdom.
21. IFAT Africa 2019: Trade Fair for Water, sewage, refuse, and recycling, on September 2019, Johannesburg, South Africa.

Bibliography

Kathpalia G.N and Rakesh Kapoor (2002). Water policy and Action plan for India 2020: An alternative (November 2002). Accessed on 23rd December 2017. www.planningcommission.nic.in/reports/genrep/bkpap2020/10_bg2020.pdf.

Standard laid down by Ministry of Environment and Forest, Government of India. Accessed on 23rd December 2017. www.mpcb.gov.in/relatedtopics/pdf/CETP

How to use secchi disk. Accessed on 3rd August 2017, http://www.rmbel.info/trainning/sechhidisk

United Nation Millinium Development Goal. Accessed on 3rd August 2017. www.un.org/millenniumgoals/environ.shtml

Sustainable Development Goal Knowledge Platform. Accessed on 3rd August 2017. http://sustainabledevelopment.un.org/sdg6

Indian National Water Policy: A review. Accessed on 21st January 2017. http://www.researchgate.net/282913105_Indian_National_water_policy_A_review

Types of wastewater treatment process: ETP, STP and CETP. Accessed on 21st January 2017. http://www.youarticlelibrary.com/water/types_of_wastewater_etp_stp_and_cetp/27418.

Water Recycling and Reuse: water/US EPA. Accessed on 24th January 2017, http://www3.epa.gov/region9/water/recycling

Agarwal Anil, Sunita Narain, and Indira Khurana (2001). Making water everybody's business. Centre for Science and Environment. ISBN: 81-86906-26-2

Birdie G.S and J.S. Birdie (2012). Water Supply and Sanitary Engineering, Volume 1, Dhanpat Rai Publishing Company (P) Ltd. ISBN: 81-87433-31-0.

Dubey R.C and D.K. Maheshwari (1999). A textbook of microbiology. Volume 1, S. Chand and Company Ltd. ISBN: 81-219-1803-0.

Sharma B.K. (2000). Environmental Chemistry. Fifth Revised and Enlarged Edition. Krishna Prakashan Media(P) Ltd. ISBN: 81-85842-84-1

Srivastava Anamika (2017). Menace of Arsenic in groundwater and its possible mitigation technologies: A Worldwide view. Volume I, Edition 1, Ideal International-e-publication. ISBN: 978-93-86675-09-5